Classroom Management for Elementary Teachers

Kim Colbert

Classroom Management for Elementary Teachers

Third Edition

CAROLYN M. EVERTSON
Peabody College, Vanderbilt University

EDMUND T. EMMER
The University of Texas, Austin

BARBARA S. CLEMENTS
Council of Chief State School Officers, Washington, D.C.

MURRAY E. WORSHAM
Northeast Independent School District, San Antonio, Texas

ALLYN AND BACON
Boston / London / Toronto / Sydney / Tokyo / Singapore

Editor-in-Chief, Education: Nancy Forsyth
Editorial Assistant: Christine Nelson
Production Administrator: Ann Greenberger
Editorial-Production Service: Progressive Typographers
Text Designer: Progressive Typographers
Cover Administrator: Linda Dickinson
Photo Researcher: Susan Duane
Manufacturing Buyer: Louise Richardson
Composition Buyer: Linda Cox

Library of Congress Cataloging-in-Publication Data
Classroom management for elementary teachers / Carolyn M. Evertson . . .
  [et al.]. — 3rd ed.
    p.   cm.
  Includes bibliographical references (p.) and index.
  ISBN 0–205–15426–3
    1. Classroom management. 2. Education, Elementary. I. Evertson,
Carolyn M.
LB3013.C528 1994
371.1′024—dc20   93–1563
                                                              CIP

Printed in the United States of America
10 9 8 7 6 5 4 3 2 1   98 97 96 95 94 93

Chapter Opening Photo Credits: Chapters 1, 2, 7, and 9: Stephen Marks
Chapters 3, 4, 5, and 6: Jim Pickerell   Chapter 8: Frank Siteman

Contents

CHAPTER 3

Managing Student Work 39

CHAPTER 4

Getting off to a Good Start 55

CHAPTER 5

Planning and Conducting Instruction 87

CHAPTER 6

Maintaining Appropriate Student Behavior   115

CHAPTER 7

Communication Skills for Teaching 133

CHAPTER 8

Managing Problem Behaviors 157

CHAPTER 9

Managing Special Groups 181

Preface

The conventional wisdom about good classroom management is that no one notices it unless it's missing. Although everyone recognizes it as one of the most important foundations of good instruction, effective classroom management doesn't just happen. Smoothly running classrooms where students are highly involved exist because teachers have clear ideas of the types of classroom conditions and student behaviors necessary for a healthy learning environment. They not only have clear ideas, but they work very hard to create these conditions. This book describes what *you* can do to create a well-managed classroom. The process is described as teachers encounter it: first by planning in several key areas before the school year begins; then by implementing the plan and establishing good management at the beginning of the year; and finally, by maintaining the management procedures throughout the year. We have tried to make the materials as useful and practical as possible by providing checklists to help you organize your planning. Several case studies and problem-solving scenarios are also provided that focus on critical areas that need special attention. We hope you will find much here that is helpful as you plan and organize for your own classroom.

This edition retains the same topics as the original book. A chapter on communication skills for teaching was added in the second edition and retained in this edition. One major change has been the addition of a new Chapter 8, "Managing Problem Behaviors," which deals with strategies you can use to intervene to restore order should it become necessary. Because not all misbehaviors are threats to your management system, this chapter helps you, first, to distinguish those behaviors that are minor from those that are serious and, second, suggests some strategies for dealing with them. Other changes made for this edition are increased coverage of topics in several of the chapters, new case studies, and updated suggestions and recommendations that reflect current research in the field.

In making these revisions, we have been influenced by our own experiences as teachers. However, most of our knowledge about classroom management derives from research and observation, both our own and others'. Our research program on classroom management extends over twenty years and has included observational studies and field experiments involving over 500 elementary and secondary classrooms. Data collected in this research are a major source of suggestions, guidelines, and case studies in this book. We therefore gratefully acknowledge our debt to many teachers who permitted us to learn from them. Without this base of reality, this book would not exist. We are also grateful to Catherine H. Randolph for her editorial help on the revisions and to the many observers, school administrators, and other researchers who both assisted and enlightened us. The authors appreciate the suggestions of Barak Rosenshine for the organization and content of the clarity section. We want to thank those who reviewed the manuscript: Marian A. Simmons, University of Missouri at Kansas City; Laverne Warner, Sam Houston State University; David M. Balzer, University of Toledo; and Suzanne Dohm.

1 Organizing Your Classroom and Supplies

Arranging the physical setting for teaching is a logical starting point for classroom management because it is a task that all teachers face before the school year begins. Many teachers find it easier to plan other aspects of classroom management after they have a clear idea of how the physical features of the classroom will be organized.

The number of things that must be considered in arranging the typical elementary school classroom is amazing! Of course, there is furniture—the teacher's and the children's desks, bookcases, filing cabinets, chairs, and a table or two. In addition, there may be audiovisual equipment such as an overhead projector, tape recorder, record player, and television. Visual aids such as bulletin boards must be prepared; charts, globes, and maps must be displayed; and storage for materials must be provided. Finally there are the personal touches that teachers often bring to a classroom, perhaps plants, an aquarium, or animal cages for hamsters. When you arrange these physical features, you will need to make many decisions. Should desks be set out in rows? Where should your desk be located?

1

Reprinted by permission: Tribune Media Services.

Where will reading groups meet with you? What areas of the room will you use for presentations? How will you and the children obtain materials and supplies?

The decisions you make will have important consequences for the success of your instructional activities. For example, if areas for storing materials are poorly placed, bottlenecks may occur when children get supplies or return them, which could slow down the activities or waste time getting them started. The location for reading groups must be chosen carefully, or you may have difficulty watching the rest of the class when meeting with a group of readers. The positioning of desks is important because a poor arrangement may interfere with visibility of chalkboards or other instructional areas, increase distractions during instruction, or make it difficult for you and your students to move around the room. Your room arrangement communicates to students how you expect them to participate in your class. Desks arranged in groups imply that interaction and collaboration among students are expected at least for some activities. Desks in rows indicate that the focus of the classroom is the teacher, the chalkboard, or some other central point. Your room arrangement should reflect your philosophy of teaching and learning.

This chapter will help you make these and other decisions about room arrangement, equipment, and basic supplies. Each component is described and guidelines and examples are given to help you plan. In addition, a checklist of room arrangement items is provided. Use it to organize your efforts in this important task and to be certain that your classroom is ready for the beginning of school.

✳ FOUR KEYS TO GOOD ROOM ARRANGEMENT ✳

Remember that the classroom is the workspace for both you and your students. It is not a very large area for up to thirty persons working for long periods of time—as much as seven hours in a day. Furthermore, you and your students will be engaging in a variety of activities and using different areas of the room. You will get good results if you arrange your room to permit orderly movement, keep distractions to a minimum, and make efficient use of available space. The following four keys will be helpful as guidelines for making decisions about your room's arrangement:

1. **Keep high traffic areas free of congestion.** Areas where many students gather and areas which receive constant use can be sites for distraction and disruption. High traffic areas include group work areas, pencil sharpener, trash can, water fountain, certain book shelves and storage areas, students' desks, and the teacher's desk. These areas should be widely separated from each other, have plenty of space, and be easy to get to.

2. **Be sure students can easily be seen by the teacher.** Careful monitoring of students is a major management task. Your success in monitoring will depend on your ability to see all students at all times. Therefore, be sure there are clear lines of sight between instructional areas, your desk, students' desks, and all student work areas. Be especially conscious of the placement of bookcases, file cabinets, and other pieces of furniture and equipment that can block your line of vision. Try standing in different parts of the room and checking for blind spots.

3. **Keep frequently used teaching materials and student supplies readily accessible.** Keeping materials accessible not only minimizes time spent getting ready and cleaning up, it also helps to avoid distracting slowdowns and breaks in the lesson flow. If you must stop during a lesson to locate needed materials and supplies, you run the risk of losing student attention and engagement. Time is lost as you must redirect attention back to the lesson. The idea of lesson flow will be discussed further in Chapter 5.

4. **Be certain students can easily see instructional presentations and displays.** Be sure that the seating arrangement will allow students to see the overhead projector screen or chalkboard without moving their chairs, turning their desks around, or craning their necks. Also, don't plan to make instructional presentations in a far corner of the room away from a substantial number of students. Such conditions do not encourage students to pay attention, and they make it more difficult for the teacher to keep all students involved in presentations and other whole-class activities. You may wish to check out how well your students can see by sitting for a moment at desks in different parts of the room.

Each of the above four keys will help produce good room arrangement. The specific components that will lead to this goal are described below. By attending to these areas you will address all of the important aspects of room arrangement. You can be confident that you will have designed a physical setting that is efficient and conducive to student involvement in work.

SUGGESTIONS FOR ARRANGING YOUR CLASSROOM

Wall and Ceiling Space

Wall space and bulletin boards provide areas to display student work, instructionally relevant material, decorative items, assignments, rules, schedules, a clock, and other items of interest. Ceiling space can also be used to hang mobiles, decorations, and student work. The following points should be considered when preparing these areas:

1. At the start of school, you should have at least the following displays for walls and chalkboards:
   Class rules (to be discussed in Chapter 2)
   A place for listing daily assignments
   Some decorative display to catch your students' interest, such as a bulletin board with a "Welcome Back to School" motif, or a display that includes the name of each child in the room.

2. Other displays that many teachers find useful include an example of the correct paper heading to be used in your class and a content-relevant display, such as one highlighting a soon-to-be-taught topic.

3. You will probably want to cover large bulletin board areas with colored paper. This paper comes on large rolls and is often kept in the school office or a supply room. You can trim the bulletin boards with an edging or border of corrugated paper. If you can't find this item in your supply room, you can spend a few dollars for the materials at a school supply center or other store. You can also find books of bulletin board ideas for sale at such stores.

4. If you need ideas for decorating your room or for setting up displays, borrow some hints from other teachers. A look in some other rooms will probably give you several new ideas.

5. *Don't* spend a lot of time decorating your room. You will have many other more important things to do to get ready for the beginning of school. A few bare bulletin boards won't bother anybody. Leave one or two empty and add displays later or allow children to decorate a blank space for an art project or as part of a science or social studies unit. Also don't over-

decorate. Wall space that is cluttered with detail can distract students and make a room seem smaller. Hanging mobiles and decorations from the ceiling can also be overdone. Your room will seem small enough when your twenty-five to thirty students are in it.

Floor Space

Arrange your furniture and equipment so that you can easily observe students from all areas of the room in which you will work. Students should be able to see you, the overhead projector screen, the main chalkboard, and any other area that will be used for presentations to the whole class. Of course, you will have to adjust to whatever constraints exist in your assigned classroom. Common problems are a classroom that is too small or that has inadequate or poorly placed chalkboard space or electrical outlets. You should assess your space and determine whatever feasible changes can be effected, within the existing constraints. For example, if the classroom is small, be sure to remove unnecessary student desks, other furniture, or equipment; if you have inadequate storage, perhaps you can locate an extra file or supply cabinet.

A good starting point for your floor plan is to determine where you will conduct whole-class instruction. Examine the room and identify where you will stand or work when you address the entire class to conduct lessons or give instructions. You can usually identify this area of the room by the location of a large chalkboard or the overhead projector screen. This area should also have room for a table or desk where you can place items needed in presentations and an electrical outlet for the overhead projector. Once you have located this area, you are ready to begin planning floor space.

As you read the following items, refer to Figure 1-1, which shows an example of a well-designed floor plan for an elementary school classroom. Note how each item has been addressed in this floor plan. Of course, this is just one of many possible alternatives. The location of desks, the small-group area, and other physical features of the classroom will depend on the size and shape of the room and how different parts of the room will be used.

Arrangement of Student Desks

Many different arrangements of student desks are possible, but be sure to arrange them so that all students can look at the whole-group instruction area without having to get out of their seats or sit with their backs to the area. Even if other arrangements are to be used later in the year, you might want to start the year with desks in rows facing the major instructional area. Children are less likely to distract each other in such an arrangement than they are when their desks are arranged in groups with children facing one another. Note that in the

Figure 1-1   An Example of a Workable Room Arrangement

classroom shown in Figure 1-1, the children's desks are arranged in clusters rather than rows; however, no child is seated with his or her back to the major instructional area. If the teacher puts a display on the overhead projector screen, all the children can see it by turning slightly in their seats and they can copy material from the screen onto their papers, at their desks.

- It is important to keep high traffic areas clear, so don't put desks or other furniture in front of doors, water fountains, sinks, the pencil sharpener, or other traffic centers. Also, try to avoid having students face potential sources of distraction, such as windows, the small-group area, animals, or other eye-catching displays.

- Be sure to leave enough room around student desks so that you can approach students to monitor them easily or give them help during seat-work activities.

- Some classrooms are equipped with tables and chairs for student seating instead of student desks. Table seating presents some special room arrangement problems, especially in grade levels higher than first and second grades. If students are seated on all sides of tables, some will have their backs to instructional presentation areas. If you have enough space and tables, this visibility problem can be avoided by seating students on only three sides of the tables. An additional problem that can be very troublesome is storage of students' supplies such as paper, notebooks, textbooks, crayons, and scissors. If there are no individual storage spaces under tables, tote trays (boxes or plastic dish tubs) may be used for students' materials. These must be stored on easily accessible shelves or carts. Plan the location of this storage area or areas carefully, for it will be used frequently and often by many students at once. Give thorough consideration to traffic patterns around and near tote tray storage areas.

■ Count the desks or chairs and make sure you have enough. Replace damaged furniture or have it repaired.

Small-Group Area

You will need an area where you can meet with small groups of children, usually for reading instruction and sometimes for math and other small-group activities. This area should be arranged so that you can observe the rest of the class from your position within the small group. Thus, your chair should be placed so that you face the whole class. Note the position of the small-group area in Figure 1-1. If you are seated facing out toward the room, you can monitor the whole class even when working with the small group. In contrast, if you were seated in the opposite chair with your back to the class, you could not see unless you turned around. Note also that there is a table in this small-group area. Although it is not required for a reading group, a table does allow this area to be used for small-group activities that include writing or working with materials.

When a table (or extra chairs) is not available, students may be asked to carry their chairs and place them in a circle (or to sit on a rug) for group instruction. An alternative is for the teacher to assign seats so that students can remain at their desks or tables for small-group instruction, while the teacher moves from group to group.

The Teacher's Desk, Filing Cabinet, Overhead Projector, and Other Equipment

Your desk needs to be placed where it is functional. If you intend to use your desk to store instructional materials, then it should be adjacent to the whole-class instructional area and preferably near any other major instructional area. If you plan to work at your desk at any time during the day, you will need to position your desk to facilitate monitoring of students. Use the same principle here as with placing the small-group area: Sit facing the students and be sure you can observe all of them from your seat. It is not necessary that students be able to see you from their seats, and some teachers prefer placing their desks at the back of the room rather than the front. If you plan to work with individual students at your desk, you will have to consider traffic patterns near your desk. Student desks should not be so close that students would be distracted by individuals approaching your desk or working with you there. Other furniture items, such as the filing cabinet and storage cabinets, also need to be where they are functional. Seldom used supplies can be safely tucked away in a corner or hidden out of view. Furniture that contains items that will be used frequently must be located near the area in which they will be used.

Bookcases

Bookcases should be placed where they will neither hinder your monitoring nor obstruct students' ability to see chalkboards or relevant displays. If the bookcases contain items that will be used frequently, such as dictionaries or supplemental readers, then the bookcases need to be conveniently located and easily monitored. If a bookcase is being used to store seldom used items, then an out-of-the-way place is best. If you have only one bookcase, try to store unneeded items in a cabinet so that the bookcase can be used for the necessary materials.

© 1968 by Bill Knowlton. Reprinted from *Classroom Chuckles* published by Scholastic Book Services.

"Come now, Miss Twist, your class isn't *that* large!"

Centers

A center is an area where students come to work on a special activity or to study some topic. Often a center will have special equipment, such as a tape recorder with headphones for individual students. Other centers may be built around a special study topic in science or social studies or around skill areas in a particular subject such as arithmetic or reading. In the latter case the teacher might include a box of activity cards that students use to progress through a series of objectives as part of enrichment or remediation. It is important to note that you do not need to have a center in your room, particularly at the beginning of the school year. There will be time enough later to introduce this feature into a classroom if you desire. If and when you do use a center, be sure to place it where you can monitor students easily. Also be certain that all necessary materials and equipment (including electrical outlets, if needed) are available at the center and functioning properly. Plan a space to post instructions for equipment use.

Pets, Plants, Aquariums, and Special Items

These can add a personal touch to a room as well as provide learning experiences for children. However, the first week of school is already quite exciting for students, so it is not necessary to introduce these special features immediately. When you do bring in such items, place them where they won't distract children, especially during whole-class activities. Of course, they should be placed where they will neither impede movement about the room nor interfere with work activities of individual students.

Storage Space and Supplies

Once you have decided on your wall and bulletin board displays and have organized space within the classroom, you can concentrate on obtaining supplies and providing for their storage. Some supplies will be used frequently and should be readily accessible. Other items will be seasonal or infrequently used and thus can go into deeper storage.

Textbooks and Other Instructional Materials

You need to identify the textbooks and other materials that are available for use in your class. Determine which books the students are allowed to keep at their desks or take home and which must remain in the room for all students to use. Then find easily accessible shelves in a bookcase for those everyday books and materials that will not be kept in student desks. If you don't know what supplemental materials are available or what the school policies are regarding these items, check with the school principal, librarian, or another teacher.

Frequently Used Classroom Materials

These are supplies that the children will use. Items included in a basic set are paper in varying sizes and colors, water-soluble markers, rulers, assorted pens and chalk for art projects, transparent tape and masking tape, stapler, and glue. These and any other supplies that are used daily should be kept at a readily accessible place, such as on a work table or shelves. Students are usually expected to supply certain materials such as pencils, erasers, pens, crayons, scissors, and notebook paper or tablets. Since you cannot count on all students bringing these materials at the beginning of the year, you should make sure you have an ample supply of these items. It is also a good idea to give parents a list of supplies that each child will need in your class.

Teacher's Supplies

You will receive some materials from the school office for your own use. These items may include pencils and pens, paper, a large, lined display tablet, chalk and erasers, overhead transparency sheets, scissors, transparent tape, ruler, stapler, paper clips, and thumbtacks. In addition, you should have a grade book, a lesson plan book, and teacher's editions for all textbooks. These items can usually be stored in your desk.

Other Materials

In addition to the items supplied by the school, a number of other supplies will come in handy. If your room does not have a clock and a calendar, obtain these now. Both should be large enough to be seen from all areas of the room. You may wish to buy a desk bell or a timer if you are going to use these as signals for starting or stopping activities. You should also add the following items: tissues, rags or paper towels, soap, bandages, and extra lunch money for emergencies. Some teachers like to keep a few basic tools such as a hammer, pliers, and screwdriver in case a minor repair needs to be made. Store all of these items where they are accessible to you but not to your students.

Student Belongings

In addition to supplies that students store in their desks or in tote trays, you need to have storage available for items such as lunch boxes, book bags, outdoor clothing, lost-and-found items, and show-and-tell materials. Leave spaces for these items as you prepare your classroom. You might wish to prepare signs designating the use to which each space will be put. Planning for student storage will help keep your classroom from becoming cluttered and will help avoid the problem of misplaced belongings.

Equipment

Check all equipment, including the overhead projector, record player, tape recorder, headphones, and pencil sharpener, to make sure they are in working order. Get any necessary extension cords or adapter plugs and store these with the equipment or in a handy place.

Seasonal or Infrequently Used Items

This category includes Halloween, Thanksgiving, and Christmas items, and any other seasonal decorations, bulletin board displays, or special project materials. Also included are instructional materials that are used only on some occasions, for example, compasses and protractors, templates, special art project materials, and science equipment. Because you do not need to have ready access to these materials, you can store them at the back of closets, in boxes on top of cabinets, or even out of the room if you have access to outside storage space.

To organize and keep track of your activities as you arrange your room, and get your equipment and supplies ready, you will find it helpful to use Checklist 1 at the end of this chapter. Each aspect of room arrangement has been listed, and space has been provided for noting what has to be done and for checking off the area once you have it ready.

SUGGESTED ACTIVITIES

The following activities will help you plan and organize your classroom space. Do as many of them as you have time for.

1. Figure 1-2 on the next page shows how one teacher arranged a classroom. There are quite a few potential problems with this room arrangement. See

Figure 1-2 A Room Arrangement with Potential Problems

how many you can find and suggest one or more ways to correct each problem. (A key for this activity is provided in the Appendix.)

2. a. Examine Figure 1-3. Based on the room arrangement, what activities would you expect to be common in this classroom? What kinds of participation will be expected from students?

   b. Picture yourself as a student in the classrooms depicted in both Figures 1-2 and 1-3. Place yourself in various areas of the room. Can you see what you need to see? Now place yourself as a teacher in the rooms. Can you see all students? Can you circulate freely among desks and work areas?

   c. The teacher whose classroom is depicted in Figure 1-3 has anticipated having twenty-eight students in her class. She has just learned that she will have at least thirty-three at the beginning of the year. How can she rearrange

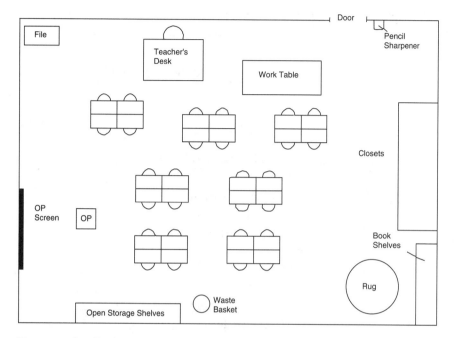

Figure 1-3 One Teacher's Planned Room Arrangement

her room to accommodate the five additional students, without losing the advantages of the arrangement she has designed?

3. Visit some other teachers' classrooms and examine their room arrangements. Use the items in Checklist 1 at the end of the chapter and the four keys to room arrangement (pp. 2–3) to guide your observation and analysis. If you are having a specific problem, ask several teachers for suggestions and look to see how they may have coped with a similar problem.

4. a. Make a scale drawing of your room, as in Figure 1-1. Use it to experiment with different furniture arrangements and the organization of space on paper, a much simpler task than pushing the furniture around yourself. Try to evaluate your arrangement using the four keys to successful room arrangement.

   b. After you have arranged the furniture in your room, test the traffic patterns from a teacher and student perspective, keeping in mind the recommendations in this chapter.

✔ CHECKLIST 1

ROOM PREPARATION

Check When Complete	Subject	Notes
☐	A. Bulletin Boards and Walls	_____
	B. Floor Space	_____
☐	1. Student desks/tables	
☐	2. Small-group area	_____
☐	3. Teacher's desk and equipment	_____
☐	4. Bookcases	_____
☐	5. Centers	_____
☐	6. Pets and plants area(s)	_____
☐	7. Traffic patterns	_____
	C. Storage Space and Supplies	
☐	1. Textbooks	_____
☐	2. Frequently used instructional materials	_____
☐	3. Teacher's supplies	_____
☐	4. Other materials	_____
☐	5. Student belongings	_____
☐	6. Equipment	_____
☐	7. Seasonal items	_____

<table>
<tr><td>

2

</td><td>

Choosing Rules and Procedures

</td></tr>
</table>

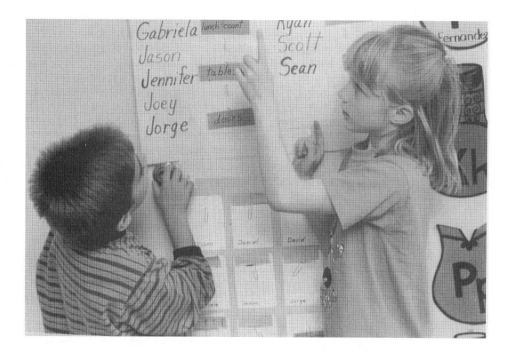

Good classroom management is based on students' understanding of the behaviors that are expected of them. A carefully planned system of rules and procedures makes it easier for you to communicate your expectations to your students, and it helps ensure that the procedures you set up will be workable and appropriate. The goal of this chapter is to help you identify a sound system of rules and procedures for your class.

Rules and procedures vary in different classrooms, but we do not find effectively managed classrooms operating without them. It is simply not possible for a teacher to conduct instruction or for students to work productively if they have no guidelines for how to behave, when to move about the room, and where to sit, or if they interrupt the teacher frequently and make whatever amount of noise pleases them. Furthermore, inefficient procedures and the absence of routines for such common aspects of classroom life as entering and leaving the room, turning in materials, participating in lessons, or checking work can waste large amounts of time and cause students' attention and interest to wane. A brief example of a classroom with major problems in the area of rules and procedures is presented below.

At 8 A.M. when the beginning-of-school bell rings, twenty-one of Ms. Smith's twenty-six fourth-grade students are in the classroom. Most are not at their desks but are milling about the room and talking noisily. Ms. Smith calls out above the din, "Everyone, sit down!" With much effort she succeeds in getting most of the children in their seats; however, three students are still standing and talking. The teacher goes to the front of the room and tries to begin a discussion of the previous day's field trip, but few children are listening. A few students straggle in at 8:06. Two others leave their seats. The teacher asks the children what they liked about their field trip. Only a few students respond. There is already some evidence of inattention: Several students are not facing the teacher, and others are quietly conversing among themselves. The teacher abandons the discussion and asks a girl to pass out some papers. At 8:09, students are sitting with nothing to do while the teacher talks with some children who have walked up to her desk. At 8:10 the teacher goes to the front of the class and announces that today she will show them something new. Two students are talking loudly, but the teacher ignores them. Three other students leave their seats: One goes to the drinking fountain, one to the pencil sharpener, and one to visit with another child. The teacher displays a definition on the overhead projector and tells students to copy it onto a piece of paper. Immediately, two students leave their seats to borrow paper, and the noise level in the room increases. About half the students get out paper. The students by the far wall are quiet, but they seem to be ignoring the teacher. One student goes to the closet, another to the pencil sharpener. Ms. Smith calls out, "Everyone, be quiet and get out some paper!" Several students call out, "What for?"

Observers of this classroom might criticize Ms. Smith for allowing students to get away with so much misbehavior. "Be stricter," they might say, "Punish the misbehaving students." Or, "Develop more interesting lessons to capture student interest." Some might even suggest that Ms. Smith set up a reward system to encourage good behavior. Although these suggestions could be helpful under some circumstances, they do not address the fundamental problem in this class-room: The students have not learned the behaviors that are expected of them. Furthermore, the teacher has not established procedures to guide student behavior. Problems are evident in several areas: the beginning-of-day routine, bringing materials for class, talking when the teacher is leading the class, out-of-seat behavior, attending to the teacher, and responding to questions.

Of course, even if the students know what is appropriate, they will not necessarily behave as they should. (For that reason this book will not end with the present chapter!) However, giving the students a clear set of expectations for what is appropriate will be a major start toward establishing a well-managed classroom environment.

Finally, keep in mind that the unique setting created by elementary school organization makes it essential to have a good set of classroom procedures. You will work with twenty-five to thirty students every day. Although your students will leave the room for lunch, recess, and perhaps some instruction, you will generally be confined to a single room with limited space and materials. You will be responsible for teaching many cognitive skills to a diverse population of students, and at the same time you will have to handle administrative tasks, arrange for appropriate materials and supplies, and evaluate students. In order to do these things well, you and your students need an orderly environment with minimal disruption and wasted time, leaving everyone free to concentrate on the critical tasks of learning. Carefully planned procedures help create this environment.

PRELIMINARY CONSIDERATIONS

Definition of Terms

Rules and *procedures* each refer to stated expectations regarding behavior. A rule identifies general expectations or standards for behavior. For example, the rule "Respect other persons and their property" covers a large set of behaviors

"This class will stimulate your ideas
and thoughts. And remember—no talking."

James Warren.

that should always be practiced. Rules frequently indicate unacceptable behavior as well as expected, appropriate behavior, although teachers sometimes manage to write rules that are only positively stated (for example, "We ask permission before talking in class"). In such instances the unacceptable behavior is implied ("Don't talk without permission"). In addition to general rules, many teachers will have a rule or two governing a specific behavior that could become an issue or that they want to prevent (for example, "Gum chewing is allowed," or "Gum chewing is not allowed").

Procedures also communicate expectations for behavior. They are usually applied in a *specific* activity, and they are usually directed at accomplishing something rather than prohibiting some behavior or defining a general standard. For example, you will set up procedures with your students for collecting assignments, turning in late work, participating in class discussions, using the bathroom, and so on. Some procedures (such as use of equipment at a center) are so sufficiently complex or critical that you may want to post guidelines in addition to discussing them with the students. However, many procedures are not written because they are very simple or because their specificity and frequency of use allow students to learn them rapidly.

Identifying School Rules and Procedures

In most schools teachers are expected to enforce a set of school rules. It is to your advantage to do so. Rules applied consistently in all classes and areas of the building are easy for students to learn. The rules also acquire more legitimacy in the eyes of some students because the rules are everyone's rules. In addition to rules and procedures that regulate student behavior, all schools have certain administrative procedures that must be followed by every teacher (for example, keeping attendance records). You should know your school's rules and procedures before the year begins so that you can also incorporate them into your own classroom system. You can find out about school rules for students and administrative procedures for teachers at a school orientation meeting or from a teacher's handbook, a building administrator, or another teacher. Pay careful attention to the following:

1. Behaviors that are specifically forbidden (examples: running in the halls, bringing certain items to school) or required (being in possession of a hall permit when out of the classroom during class time, bringing a note for absence).

2. Consequences for rule violations. In particular, you need to note the responsibility you have for carrying out the consequence, such as reporting the student to the school office. If the school does not have a policy for

dealing with certain rule violations, then you will need to decide how to handle them yourself.

3. Administrative procedures that must be handled during class time. These procedures include beginning-of-year tasks such as assigning textbooks to students, collecting fees, and checking the class roster. Money collection (for school lunches, for example) will go on all year, so you will need some system of record keeping and a safe place to keep the money. Some administrative tasks will have to be conducted each day. These include taking and recording class attendance in your grade book, handling previously absent students, and filing an attendance report with the office. You will also need a procedure for allowing students to leave the room to go to other parts of the building. Frequently, procedures in these areas will already be established and followed throughout the school. If uniform procedures have not been implemented in the school in some area, you may find it helpful to talk with experienced teachers about how they handle it.

Planning Your Classroom Rules

Once you have information about school rules and procedures, you will be ready to begin planning for your own classroom. Guidelines for rules will be presented separately from those for procedures.

Many different rules are possible, but a set of five to eight rules should be sufficient to cover most important areas of behavior. Five general rules that

© 1968 by Bill Knowlton. Reprinted from *Classroom Chuckles* published by Scholastic Book Services.

encompass many classroom behaviors are listed below. These or similar rules are often found in well-managed classrooms, although we do not intend that they be considered a definitive list. You may decide to use other rules (for example, a rule prohibiting a specific behavior) or different wording. Some teachers may find these rules too general, and they might prefer to have more rules with greater specificity. After each rule are some examples of behaviors related to the rule. When presenting general rules, it is important to discuss your specific expectations with students. When discussing the rules and related behaviors, it is best to emphasize the positive parts of the rules, rather than just their negative counterparts. When you do the former, you help students learn how to behave appropriately. You will need to be explicit about behaviors that are not acceptable when such behaviors might occur frequently (examples would be gum chewing, being out of seat, call-outs). These may be incorporated into your set of rules or discussed when presenting procedures associated with specific activities. Be sure your presentation includes concrete examples and that you explain any terms that the children at your grade level might not understand.

The set of rules you choose will be used later in several ways. First, you will discuss these rules with your students on the first day or two of class. You will also post the rules in the room and/or make certain that students have their own copies. A posted set of rules allows you to focus student attention on and create a strong expectation about behaviors that are important to you. Finally, you may refer to specific rules as needed to remind students of appropriate behavior during the year. It should be noted that your posted rules need not (and cannot) cover all aspects of behavior in detail. Procedures for specific activities and perhaps some ad hoc rules will be needed. For instance, you may wish to post separately your policies regarding student work. Examples of some commonly used rules follow.

RULE 1. BE POLITE AND HELPFUL. This may be worded in various ways (e.g., be considerate of others, be courteous). For the rule to have meaning, the children must be given examples: Wait your turn; say "please" and "thank-you"; behave properly for a substitute. Some "don'ts" could include fighting, name calling, and bothering others.

RULE 2. RESPECT OTHER PEOPLE'S PROPERTY. This rule may include guidelines such as (a) keep the room clean and neat; (b) pick up litter; (c) return borrowed property; (d) do not write on the desks; and (e) do not use another person's things without permission.

RULE 3. LISTEN QUIETLY WHILE OTHERS ARE SPEAKING. Use of this rule will prevent call-outs and other interruptions of lessons. You can use the discussion of this rule to teach the students how to comment or ask a question (e.g., raise a hand and wait to be called on).

RULE 4. RESPECT AND BE POLITE TO ALL PEOPLE.   This rule is general, so be sure to give sufficient examples and explanation so that both you and students clearly understand its meaning. You will need to define *polite,* and you may want to extend this definition to include not hitting, fighting, or name calling. You may also want to emphasize that "all people" includes you, the teacher.

RULE 5. OBEY ALL SCHOOL RULES.   Including this rule gives you an opportunity to discuss whatever school rules are pertinent to your supervision of students outside of your classroom (such as on the playground or in the cafeteria). It reminds students that school rules apply in your classroom as well as out of it. It also suggests that you will monitor their behavior in the areas covered by the school rules.

Student Participation in Rule Setting

Some teachers involve students in rule setting in order to promote ownership of the rules and to encourage them to take more responsibility for their own behavior. Student involvement can take many forms, such as a discussion focused on reasons for having rules and on clarifying the rationale for and the meaning of particular rules. A discussion might begin with a consideration of why rules are necessary. After this initial discussion, rules can be presented one at a time. The teacher may first clarify the rule by describing (or asking students to describe) the area of behavior it covers. Students can usually supply concrete examples, although they will tend to give negative instances, such as "Respecting property means not marking on desks or not stealing." Consequently, you should be prepared to state some positive examples. The discussion of individual rules may also include a rationale for those rules whose justification is not obvious.

Another way to involve students in rule setting is to allow them to share in the decision-making process for specific rules. This is sometimes done at a school level (mainly in the intermediate grades) by having student representatives from each room or grade level participate in the identification of school rules. However, within individual classrooms shared decision making is not very common for several possible reasons. First, the domain in which student participation is acceptable is limited. Schoolwide rules must be accepted as they are. Second, policies that are essential to managing instruction cannot be left to student discretion. Finally, elementary age students may require considerable prompting to produce a comprehensive list of general rules. Thus, most teachers prefer to develop and present their rules, including students in a discussion of examples and rationales.

Another approach taken by some teachers is to limit student choice issues to particular activities or behaviors. For example, if gum chewing is not prohibited by a school rule and if you do not find it objectionable, then you could give your students a choice. It would be a rare class that decided to prohibit it! When students are given a choice, then you must also make them aware of their responsibility for making the chosen procedure or rule work and remind them they will lose the privilege if their behavior warrants it.

It is important to note that many effective managers do not provide for student choice in rule setting. Instead, they clearly present their rules and procedures to students and provide explanations of the need for them. A teacher who establishes reasonable rules and procedures, who provides an understandable rationale for them, and who enforces them consistently will find that the great majority of students are willing to abide by them.

PLANNING CLASSROOM PROCEDURES

If you have never analyzed the specific behaviors required of students in a typical elementary school classroom, you are going to be surprised by the complexity and detail in this section. Don't hurry through it, even though some of the items may appear trivial. These bits and pieces will combine to form the mosaic of your management system. Five categories of procedures are described: procedures for room areas, procedures for teacher-led instruction and seatwork activities, transitions into and out of the room, procedures for small-group work, and general procedures. A sixth area, dealing with keeping students accountable for work, is presented in Chapter 3.

As you read the items below, note ideas for procedures on Checklist 2.

Procedures for Room Use

Different areas of the room and furniture and equipment within the room need procedures to regulate their use.

☆ Teacher's Desk and Storage Areas

The best procedure is that students may not remove anything from your desk or other storage areas without your permission.

Student Desks and Other Student Storage Areas

Just as students may not tamper with your desk, students may not bother the desk or storage space of another student. You can also help students learn good work habits by setting aside a few minutes each week for students to clean out and organize their desks and materials. This is a good end-of-day activity on Friday.

Storage for Common Materials

Some commonly used supplies (scissors, scrap paper, rulers, etc.) and resources (supplementary books, basals, encyclopedia, dictionaries, etc.) will be stored on shelves, in drawers, or in cabinets. Most teachers label these storage areas appropriately and tell students at what times these materials may be used and whether permission is needed for any of them.

Drinking Fountain, Sink, Pencil Sharpener

A common procedure is to allow use of these by only one student at a time and only when the teacher is not conducting a lesson or talking to the whole class. Some teachers require students to request permission to use the fountain or sink except during specified break times.

Bathrooms

When bathrooms are immediately accessible from or adjacent to the classroom, many teachers allow students to use these facilities, one at a time, without asking permission whenever the teacher is not conducting instruction. A system should be established to let a student know if the bathroom is occupied (examples: a reversible sign on the door with a green light and a red light; knocking and waiting). It is also a good idea to go over bathroom use procedures, such as flush toilet, wash hands, wipe off sink area, and dispose of paper towels.

Centers, Stations, and Equipment Areas

Procedures that need to be established include when the area may be used (perhaps after other work is finished or during particular lessons only), whether special permission is needed, and how many may use the area at a time. Teachers often allow quiet talking in such areas as long as it does not disturb others. If talking will be allowed, then the area should be situated away from the rest of the class. Post rules or instructions for equipment use at each area.

Procedures During Seatwork and Teacher-Led Activities

Good procedures for these activities are especially important because it is during these times that instruction and learning take place. Major concerns include keeping student attention, regulating participation, and providing assistance when needed. Good procedures will prevent or reduce interruptions or distractions that can slow down content development activities or interfere with student learning.

Student Attention During Presentations

It is important to consider how students should behave when you are presenting information to the class or while you are conducting a presentation or recitation. Typically, students are expected to face the teacher and listen attentively. In fact, teachers often translate this expectation into a general classroom rule such as "Listen carefully when the teacher or another student is talking." Teachers also expect students to remain seated at all times during presentations and not engage in social conversation, and to have only the books or other materials needed for the lesson on their desks.

Student Participation

You will need to identify some procedure to enable students to ask a question, contribute to a discussion, or receive help. During presentations and discussions, the simplest procedure is to require that students raise their hands, wait to be called on, and remain in their seats. In most circumstances it is not a good idea to allow students to call out answers or comments without raising their hands. Undesirable consequences of allowing call-outs include domination of participation by a few students, frequent inappropriate comments, and interruptions of discussions and presentations. Requiring that students raise their hands gives all students an opportunity to participate and allows you to call on students who do not have their hands up, if you choose. Two exceptions to the "no call-out" procedure are sometimes permitted. The first occurs when teachers want students to provide a chorus response; that is, when they want a whole class response to a question. This can be handled by telling students at the beginning of the activity that they do not need to raise their hands to respond. Also children can be taught a signal for a chorus response; cupping one hand behind an ear or giving a verbal signal, such as prefacing the question with "everyone," can be used. A second exception may occur during activities in which hand raising might slow down or interfere with a discussion. Again, students can be told that it is not necessary to raise hands during that particular activity. It is worth noting that the variations from the standard procedure of requiring raised hands usually should not be used early in the school year. Instead, follow a simple routine for several weeks until you are certain that students understand it. Then, if you choose to depart from the procedure, clearly communicate the difference to the students at the beginning of the activity.

Talk Among Students

Although student talk during teacher presentations is not allowed, some effective classroom managers allow quiet talking between students during seat-work activities when such talk is content related. In many activities, quiet talk is an important part of problem-solving. However, students must know when and how loudly they may talk. You will have to decide what your policy will be and communicate it to the students. The "no talking" rule is easier to monitor, and you may want to start with this procedure during the first month or so of the school year. Then try allowing students to help each other on a trial basis. If you decide to allow students to talk to one another and to work together during seatwork activities, you will need to establish specific limitations. For example, you might tell students that during certain activities quiet talking is allowed, but if it gets too loud, the privilege will be lost. It would be best to demonstrate what "quiet talking" means and have students practice it to show you they know what is meant.

Obtaining Help

When students are working at their seats and need help, you should have them raise their hands. It is not a good idea to allow them to call out or to come up to you whenever they wish. Once they have raised their hands, you may then go to them or have them come to you one at a time. Another procedure is to allow students to come up only if you are seated at your desk (or some other designated place) and not already helping another student. These procedures will eliminate long lines of chatty students around your desk. They will also allow you to control where you give individual assistance. If you choose to help students at a location other than their desks, choose one that allows you good visibility of the rest of the class.

Out-of-Seat Procedures

To eliminate unnecessary wandering around the room, you should indicate when students are allowed to leave their seats. For example, students may sharpen pencils, turn in papers, and get supplies only when necessary and you are not talking to the class. The "one at a time" rule should be enforced.

When Seatwork Has Been Completed

Sometimes one or several students will finish their seatwork before the next scheduled activity. This situation is frequently handled either by having students complete an additional, enrichment assignment, or by allowing these students to use the remaining time for free reading or work at a center or to help with classroom maintenance chores. You may also wish to have some students who finish early serve as peer tutors for others. If you have enrichment activities that involve additional materials not in the students' possession, you will need to specify when these materials may be used, where they will be kept, and what the procedures are for returning the materials to the proper place. Note that if many students frequently complete their work early, it is evidence that assignments are insufficient or too much time is being allocated for seatwork activities.

Transitions Into and Out of the Room

Beginning the School Day

You should establish a routine to open each class day. This routine should be supervised and led by you so that it is done efficiently and helps students "settle in" to the classroom. The routine need not be elaborate or time-consuming. Many teachers begin with social items such as a riddle for the day, a discussion of the day's lunch menu, the pledge of allegiance, date and birthdays, discussion of school events, or other items of interest. Not only does this routine establish a whole-class focus, it also gives the students a chance to get some of their chatter out of the way before beginning academic content activities. It also lets late students arrive before lessons begin or instructions for assignments are given. You may also wish to hand back graded papers or collect money, permission slips, or other items brought from home at this time. If much time will be required for morning management tasks, have students begin work on a content-related activity to establish an academic focus to be sure students are not in dead time.

Leaving the Room

Your students will leave the room en masse at several times during the day: at recess and for lunch, physical education, music, or perhaps some other instruction. A common technique used is to have the children line up after appropriate materials have been put away, with the quietest table or row lining up first. Decide what behaviors are appropriate in line. Some teachers, particularly of younger children, find it necessary to specify where hands and feet should be while students are lined up. Some teachers have students clasp their hands behind their backs; others have students keep their hands at their sides. Line leaders can be helpful and students enjoy the privilege. Because noise would disturb other classes, talking is usually forbidden while the line is passing through the halls. You will also need procedures for helping students in pull-out programs know when and how to leave the room.

Returning to the Room

Frequently teachers establish a procedure for this transition, particularly after lunch time. A common one is as follows: Students are to enter the room quietly and take their seats; they may read or rest with their heads on their desks; students who need to use the bathroom, sink, pencil sharpener, or drinking fountain may do so, one at a time at each area. Note that this procedure gets students ready for afternoon activities. At times other than lunch, a common procedure is to return immediately to one's seat and stay there with no talking or perhaps whispering only until the teacher begins the next activity.

When students return from an out-of-room activity that has left them noisy or unusually "chatty," or if they are very excited when returning from recess or lunch, your transition activity should give them time to wind down before you start academic work. For example, you might permit quiet social talk as they settle in and get ready for the next lesson. Some research has found that student attention is better after such transitions than when the teacher tries to enforce total silence and an immediate return to academic tasks. However, do not prolong the chatter unnecessarily, and be sure to gain student attention when you begin the next activity. Monitor students so that "wind down" time doesn't become "wind up" time.

Ending the Day

A routine is needed at the end of the day to ensure that the students' desks and work areas are cleared off, materials to go home are ready, and students leave on time. Planning ahead for the end of the day guards against hurried closings, lost papers, and a feeling of confusion and chaos. Possible routines include feeding room pets, straightening bookshelves, tidying up desks, and stacking chairs on the desks. Other important end-of-day tasks include briefly reviewing important things learned that day, foreshadowing coming events, and checking materials that will be taken home. If you have children who leave early to ride a bus, you may wish to do only the essentials with them and complete the rest of the routine after they leave.

Procedures During Reading and Other Small-Group Activities

One complication with using small-group instruction is that the teacher is often working with one group while the rest of the class is engaged in individual seatwork. The dual focus complicates monitoring, providing assistance, and dealing with problems that might occur. Well-planned procedures are a must if small-group instruction is to be carried out smoothly.

Getting the Class Ready for the Activity

Students must know what work they are going to do during the time they are not in the group. Therefore, you must post the seatwork assignments by group and discuss work requirements beforehand with the whole class. You should also note any materials that will be needed when the students come to the reading group.

Student Movement Into and Out of the Group

These transitions need to be brief, quiet, and free from disruptions. Describe expected behavior to students: walk, no talking, bring needed materials. You will need a signal to tell students when to come up to the group area. They should not automatically come when they see other students leave, because you may want to check on student progress before working with the next group. Some teachers use a bell or a kitchen timer; others just use a verbal signal.

Expected Behavior of Students in the Group

The rules for attention and hand raising used in the whole class can also be used in the small group. However, with smaller numbers of students, some procedures must change, and these must be taught. For example, some teachers have each student who responds select the next student to participate.

Expected Behavior of Students Not in the Small Group

You will have given instructions to students not in the group and posted their seatwork assignments. However, students may need help as they work. It is not a good idea to allow students to come up to you while you are in the group; therefore, some procedure must be established to enable students to get help. One such procedure is to allow students to help each other. Another procedure used by some teachers is to assign certain students the job of monitors. Students can then raise their hands and the monitor can go to assist them. Permission to interrupt the teacher is then given only to the monitors and only when assistance is absolutely necessary. Often, students are told that they should skip the part of the assignment they are unable to do and that the teacher will help them later. You should check on student progress even while you are working with the group. Look up frequently to scan the class for signs of difficulty. Then when you change groups, circulate around the room to help students before you call the next group. Students can raise their hands between groups to indicate a need for help, or they may write their names on the chalkboard to signal a need for assistance when you are available.

Learning Teams

An instructional method that makes extensive use of groups is the use of learning teams or cooperative learning groups. This method has been applied widely in many subjects and grade levels. Typically, teams are formed hetero-geneously and work on academic tasks requiring cooperation. Cooperation among team members within groups is encouraged through incentives; teams may compete against each other and be rewarded on the basis of group perform-ance. Although procedures for organizing learning teams are similar to those described previously for the use of small groups, there are some unique charac-teristics. If you plan to use them, some good source books are by Slavin, Sharan, Kagan, Hertz-Lazarowitz, Webb, and Schmuck (1985) and Johnson and Johnson (1986).

General Procedures

Distributing Materials

At the beginning of the year books and supplies must be distributed to students. You will need some procedures for recording book numbers, noting damage, and handling some other details. These will be covered in Chapter 4 along with other procedures for beginning the school year. In addition to the beginning-of-year materials distribution, you will have supplies, papers, and books to pass out every day. Unless you establish efficient procedures, a lot of time can be wasted doing this. Many teachers have student helpers pass out materials such as dittos, workbooks, or graded papers during opening activities. For the distribution of books or supplies, a student helper can be assigned to each table or row. If you collect papers from assignments by group or by row and preserve the order while you are checking them, you can then redistribute them to the class in the same way. This makes it easy to hand the materials to one student at each table or in each row.

Interruptions or Delays

If delays or interruptions occur while students are working, they should be taught to continue their work silently. Tell students that they should be courteous and patient if you are interrupted in the middle of a lesson by a visitor or a phone call and that you will return to them as quickly as possible. If you will be detained very long, give the students something to do in case they finish their work before you return.

Bathrooms

If bathrooms are located away from your classroom, a hall-pass system may be established to monitor the number of students out of the room and to let students know if they may leave. You might hang a bathroom hall pass next to the hall door to be placed by the student around his or her neck or carried en route to the bathroom. There may already be a schoolwide procedure, so be certain you know what it is.

Library, Resource Room, School Office

When one or a small group of students must go to another area in the school, you will generally remain in the classroom with the rest of the students. School-wide procedures are usually established to handle these situations. Find out whether a hall permit system or some other procedure is used to regulate movement of students in the halls. Also review any school rules that govern behavior in transit or at the locations. You will want to make sure your students understand these procedures.

Cafeteria

Review the school policies for the cafeteria and be ready to explain them to your class before they go to lunch and after they return if needed. If you are planning to (or must) sit with the students, decide ahead of time who will get to sit by you and whether this will be at random, a privilege, or whether you will use assigned seats. If your students are too noisy or misbehave, you may wish to establish a reward system for good behavior or include lunchroom behavior as part of your in-class reward system.

Playground

Safety rules are a must, and you should limit overly aggressive behavior and dangerous play. Also if any of the equipment in the playground poses a potential hazard, you will need to talk about it with your students. Make clear to your students what part of the school grounds they may use for recess. You also should establish some signal for getting students' attention when it is time for them to line up and return to the classroom; this could be a whistle or a raised hand. If you plan to play a game on the playground, announce this prior to leaving the room, telling students where they should go once out on the playground.

Fire and Disaster Drills

You need to find out what school policies and routines have been established to protect the children and you. While you may wish to wait a while before teaching these to your students, you should not wait until you know a drill is imminent. It is better to go over these procedures ahead of time and then review them just prior to the first drill.

Classroom Helpers

Teachers often use students to help with such chores as erasing the chalkboard, passing out materials and supplies, carrying messages to the office, watering the plants, and feeding the animals. Students are often chosen to be line leaders and classroom monitors. Some teachers use these activities as privileges or rewards for especially good or improved behavior, or they may use them to encourage some students to accept more responsibility. Some teachers have a chart or bulletin board with slots for the names of students currently serving as monitors or helpers. A card is then made for each child with his or her name, and this card is placed in the appropriate slot when that child has a particular room helper responsibility. Some teachers ask for volunteers for each job; others appoint students on a rotating basis or use jobs as rewards. Appointment is usually done at the beginning of the week and the appointments last one or two weeks.

SUGGESTED ACTIVITIES

1. Identify the schoolwide rules and procedures that you and your students are expected to observe. Be sure these are incorporated into your own classroom rules and procedures where appropriate.

2. Read Case Studies 2-1 and 2-2 on the following pages. They illustrate classroom procedures and rules for most major areas, and they will help you develop your own system of management.

3. Case Study 2-3 illustrates a more complex classroom organization involving introducing multiple areas and centers for student activities. List some of the

advance planning decisions Ms. Miller has made. What rules and procedures has she developed? How are these taught and monitored?

4. Use Checklist 2 at the end of this chapter to help organize your planning of classroom procedures. Be sure to think through your expectations for student behavior in each of the general areas and the instructional areas that you will be using. Then develop a set of procedures that will communicate your expectations to your students.

5. If you have trouble developing procedures in some area or are not sure if the ones you have identified will work, be sure to ask other teachers for their opinions. They will usually be more than happy to share some of their "tricks of the trade."

6. Develop a list of five to eight general classroom rules. Be sure these emphasize areas of classroom behavior that are important to you and to the functioning of your classroom. Review these with an administrator or another teacher.

CASE STUDY 2-1

Classroom Procedures and Rules in a Second-Grade Class. Ms. Able's students followed four rules: We are quiet in the classroom. We do our best work. We are polite and helpful. We follow all school rules. Students were taught that being quiet in the classroom meant that they usually had a choice of being silent or talking in whisper voices. When the teacher was addressing the class or when she told the class to be silent, students were to stop their whispers and be silent. Most of the time, however, students were allowed to work together, whispering. If a student was loud, the student lost the whisper privilege and had to be silent.

The rule "We do our best work" included listening carefully when the teacher was giving instructions, completing all assignments, turning in neat work, and making good use of time in class.

Student behaviors relating to the rule "We are polite and helpful" included taking turns in class and raising hands to receive permission to talk. Ms. Able explained to her students that in order for everyone to have a chance to talk and to be heard, they should raise their hands and wait to be called on when they wanted to answer a question or make a comment. Other aspects of consideration and respect for fellow students, the teacher, and other adults in the school were also included under this rule. In addition, the school rules referred to in the fourth classroom rule governed student behavior in the halls, cafeteria, and other common areas of the school grounds.

Several other important classroom procedures provided guidelines for student behavior in Ms. Able's classroom. Students were expected to stay seated at their desks whenever the teacher was presenting directions or instruction to the class as a whole. At other times, however, Ms. Able's students were allowed to leave their desks to get supplies, hand in papers, sharpen their pencils, and use the restroom that was adjacent to the classroom, without asking the teacher's permission as long as they did not disturb other students. For example, students were allowed to sharpen a pencil without permission except when the teacher was talking to the class or when another student was addressing the class. No more than two students were allowed at the pencil sharpener at one time, one sharpening and one waiting. When the teacher was working with a small group or helping an individual, students were not allowed to walk up to her or interrupt. They stayed at their desks and raised their hands to request assistance. If students finished their work early, they were allowed to read their library books, work a dittoed puzzle, or play an instructional game. They could talk, using their whisper voices, but they could not disturb anyone still working on the assignment. Unless they had permission to do otherwise, they were expected to stay at their own desks.

When Ms. Able needed to get the attention of the class, she routinely used a bell as a signal. She taught students that when she rang the bell once they were to immediately be silent and look at her. She explained to the class that using the bell was a shortcut to save time, that she would ring the bell only once and not several times, and that she expected students to respond immediately. She used the bell in a very consistent manner.

CASE STUDY 2-2

Small-Group Procedures.   At the end of the second week of school, Ms. Bernal announced to her fourth-grade class that they would be doing two new things that day: working independently and reading in small groups. She defined the word *independently* as doing their own work without interrupting other students. She then called students' attention to a group of exercises on the front board. These were spelling and language arts activities that the teacher knew students could do on their own. She gave directions for each exercise, step by step, doing the first of each type of activity as an example. She questioned students to be sure they understood what to do and gave them ample time and encouragement to ask questions. The teacher reemphasized that they were to work independently and told them that now was their last opportunity to ask questions before their reading group met. She told students to skip an exercise if they could not do it and go back to it after they received help.

Ms. Bernal then reminded the class that students could go to the bathroom one at a time, except when she was talking to the whole class. She announced that while she was working with reading groups that day, students not in the reading group could use the bathroom, wash hands, sharpen one pencil, or get a drink of water if necessary while they were doing seatwork. She then asked if there were any questions. There were none. She asked one child to repeat to the class what they were to do when not in a small reading group.

Ms. Bernal called out the names of the Green group members, then had them raise their hands. Then she did the same with the Yellow group and the Red group. She pointed to a small bulletin board where the names of the students in each group were posted below the group's color name. The groups would be called in the order on the bulletin board: Red, Yellow, then Green. The signal to come to group would be the timer bell. Each group would last about twenty minutes. Students were told to stack their books and papers quickly and neatly on their desks when they were called to reading group. They did not have to bring any materials to the reading group because the teacher would provide the things they would need. Ms. Bernal stressed that she expected the students to be very quiet coming to and leaving the reading circle, so as not to disturb students working at their desks. She told the class that she was very interested in hearing every student read, and this would be impossible if there were a lot of talking and noise.

Ms. Bernal then told the children that if they finished their seatwork, they were to take out library books and read quietly. She asked a member of each group to restate the instructions for each seatwork assignment to be sure that her expectations for the group were understood. When she was sure that everyone knew how to get started, she asked the Red group to come to the reading circle and told the rest of the students to go to work on the board work. The Red group moved quickly to the reading circle as the teacher waited and watched them and the rest of the class, making sure that students in the Yellow and Green groups were starting their work. She paid special attention to students in the Yellow group (her lowest-performing readers), who were more likely to need help getting started on their assignments. The teacher's chair was placed in the reading circle so that she could monitor the entire class while she was teaching the small group. Once she noticed three students talking at their seats. She stopped work in the small group to remind the class briefly that she wanted complete silence during reading group and that she was watching for students who were particularly good at following directions. Later during reading group, several students raised their hands and looked toward the teacher. She noticed the hands, caught the students' eyes, and shook her head. This was a signal to these students that it was inappropriate to ask questions while the teacher was in reading group.

When the Red group's time was almost up, the teacher reminded them of her instructions about what they were to do at their desks and told them that she would check over their work after finishing with the second group, the Yellow group (who were the slower readers). With that she sent the Red group to their seats and rang the timer bell. She watched as students in the Yellow group left their desks and came to the reading circle while the Red group began seatwork. She complimented the students in the Yellow reading group for walking quietly and leaving their books stacked neatly. She answered the seatwork questions of the Red and Green groups before proceeding with the rest of the morning's reading activities.

Ms. Bernal planned her group schedule to support the needs of each group of students. She met with the slower readers (the Yellow group) second because these students sometimes had trouble concentrating on seatwork for an extended period. Meeting with them second meant that their seatwork was split into two short sessions (before and after their meeting with her) rather than one long session. She met with the highest performing group last, because they were most able to interpret and complete their seatwork assignments independently.

Later during the year, Ms. Bernal introduced new activities in the reading group routine, such as listening center activities or language skill box exercises. Groups rotated from seatwork to reading group to some other activity. Each change in class routine was carefully planned and explained to the students so that they were able to participate in the activities in an orderly way as Ms. Bernal conducted reading instruction in the small groups.

CASE STUDY 2-3

Using Centers in a Multitask Classroom. Ms. Miller had designed her upper elementary classroom with centers for listening, reading, writing, and creating. Special interest centers on topics the class is studying in science, social studies, or math change every month or so. Although each child has a desk, students are seldom in their seats; instead, they work on a variety of projects individually, in pairs, and in groups. When they meet as a whole class, they often gather sitting on a carpet instead of in traditional rows of desks. On any given day in November, a visitor may see an active, busy, somewhat noisy place, but it takes only a few minutes to discern that there is a sense of order and purpose to the tasks in which the students are engaged.

This classroom didn't get this way all at once. Much of the first six weeks of school were spent preparing students to work independently and collaboratively. On the first day of school, Ms. Miller taught students cues for when to gather on the rug and when to return to seats. She explained that there would be times when they could talk to each other, but that during "rug time" they were to raise their hands so that only one person would be speaking at once. Ms. Miller had prepared a poster with the day's schedule and "center time" clearly marked. She went over it with the students before posting it on a highly visible bulletin board. She made a habit of referring to the poster during the first weeks of school when giving students instructions for activities, or she asked students to tell her when certain activities were to start or stop.

Centers were introduced one at a time, over a period of several weeks. When each new center became available, Ms. Miller presented it to the whole class, demonstrating the material found there and pointing out times on the day's schedule when it would be available. She also pointed out two signs in each center. One sign lists the procedures for the center. For example, the sign in the reading center says, "Silent readers may leave the center to find a quiet place to read. Students reading aloud to each other should stay in the center." Every list of procedures ends with instructions for clean-up. The second sign lists the capacity of that center. For example, the listening center has only four sets of earphones, so its capacity is four. Ms. Miller explains to the students that they may sign up for centers each morning when they arrive at school. One period of the day is allotted to "free center time," when students may go to the centers they have chosen. During free center time, students cross their names off the sign-up sheets when they leave the center, so other students may enter. Another period is "assigned center time," when Ms. Miller decides who should be in each center. After each new center is introduced, Ms. Miller makes sure that every student visits it during assigned center time. She monitors the center's use carefully, making sure that all students understand the use of one center before another center is introduced. Even after all centers have been introduced, Ms. Miller continues to monitor their use and brings up any common problems she sees for discussion during rug time. She is careful to balance the available centers so that if activities at one center require her attention, the other centers have more familiar activities available, on which students can work independently.

✔ CHECKLIST 2

RULES AND PROCEDURES

Check When Complete	Subject	Procedures or Expectations
	Room use	
☐	A. Teacher's desk and storage areas	_____
☐	B. Student desks and storage areas	_____
☐	C. Storage for common materials	_____
☐	D. Drinking fountains, sink, pencil sharpener	_____
☐	E. Bathrooms	_____
☐	F. Centers, stations, or equipment areas	_____
☐	G. Chalkboard	_____
	Seatwork and Teacher-Led Instruction	
☐	A. Student attention during presentations	_____
☐	B. Student participation	_____
☐	C. Talk among students	_____
☐	D. Obtaining help	_____
☐	E. Out-of-seat procedures during seatwork	_____
☐	F. When seatwork has been completed	_____
	Transitions Into and Out of the Room	
☐	A. Beginning the school day	_____
☐	B. Leaving the room	_____
☐	C. Returning to the room	_____
☐	D. Ending the day	_____

Check When Complete	Subject	Procedures or Expectations
	Procedures during Reading or Other Groups	
☐	A. Getting the class ready	_____
☐	B. Student movement	_____
☐	C. Expected behavior in the group	_____
☐	D. Expected behavior of students out of group	_____
	General Procedures	
☐	A. Distributing materials	_____
☐	B. Classroom helpers	_____
☐	C. Interruptions or delays	_____
☐	D. Bathrooms	_____
☐	E. Library, resource room, school office	_____
☐	F. Cafeteria	_____
☐	G. Playground	_____
☐	H. Fire and disaster drills	_____

3 Managing Student Work

When we presented a set of procedures for establishing an orderly classroom setting in Chapter 2, we also indicated that additional procedures would be needed to keep students accountable for their work. In this chapter we will describe the additional procedures, which are aimed at encouraging students to complete assignments and to engage in other learning activities.

Each day of the school year you will give your students assignments that they will be expected to complete in the classroom or at home. These assignments are important for learning and retention because they provide systematic practice, the application of knowledge, and repeated exposure to content. Thus, the consistent and accurate completion of assignments is a critical goal for effective management. If students are not held accountable for their work, many problems in this area can occur. Consider the following hypothetical example:

During the second month of school, Mr. Paul is beginning to notice several disturbing signs of a lack of interest in assignments on the part of a number of his fourth-grade students. This is most evident during reading groups and in math.

When Mr. Paul meets with reading groups in the morning, he usually gives students who are not in the group two assignments to do as seatwork. Generally one of these is a worksheet activity related to the reading assignment and the other is a language arts activity such as spelling practice or handwriting. Early in the year, Mr. Paul had much trouble with interruptions during the reading group as students left their seats and came up for directions and help. He put a stop to that by enforcing a rule prohibiting "come ups," but now students are talking constantly during seatwork. When Mr. Paul checks on their progress at the completion of reading group time, as many as half the students have hardly begun their assignments or are doing them carelessly and incorrectly.

In math after a presentation of the material for the day, Mr. Paul usually gives an assignment. If students do not complete the work in class, then they are expected to take it home and complete it there. Mr. Paul usually lets students check their own work, and he picks up work and grades it about once a week. During the last several of these weekly checks, he has discovered that four or five students are not doing the assignment and at least as many have incomplete papers with many errors.

It is apparent that many of Mr. Paul's students do not feel very accountable for their work. It is possible, of course, that some of the assignments are too difficult or are not explained adequately, but it is also very likely that many of Mr. Paul's procedures are not helping the students develop good work habits or learn the importance of prompt and accurate completion of assignments. The basis for the poor student effort could be determined from answers to the following questions:

- Are the required standards for quality and amount of work clear to the students?

- Is student progress being monitored closely?

- What kinds of feedback do students receive about their progress as well as about their completed work? How immediate is the feedback?

- What are the consequences for incomplete or careless student work?

- What are the incentives for careful and prompt completion of assignments?

Important areas of accountability are addressed by these questions, and in each area Mr. Paul could do several things to encourage students to complete assignments promptly and correctly. This chapter will focus on aspects of classroom procedures that communicate the importance of work assignments, that enable students to understand what is expected of them, and that help them make good progress. The critical areas include communicating assignments and work requirements, monitoring student progress, and providing feedback. Checklist 3 is provided to help organize your planning in these areas. In addition, three case studies of accountability systems of elementary teachers are provided at the end of the chapter.

CLEAR COMMUNICATION OF ASSIGNMENTS AND WORK REQUIREMENTS

Students need a clear idea of what their assignments are and what is expected of them. This means that you must be able to explain all requirements and features of the assignments. Verbal explanation alone will not be sufficient because not all students listen carefully, some students may be absent when the assignments and requirements are discussed, and the assignment itself may be complex. In addition, there is more to completing assignments than doing the work accurately. You must also consider standards for neatness, legibility, and form. While we do not want to encourage an overemphasis on form to the detriment of the content objectives, some standards in these areas must be set. The following three areas should be considered.

Instructions for Assignments

In addition to telling the students what the assignment is, you should routinely post the assignment and important instructions on a chalkboard, overhead projector, or flip chart. It is also a good idea to teach students to copy the assignment into their notebooks or on the first line of their papers so they will have a record of it if they need it to complete work at home. Go over instructions orally with the class, indicating where they are displayed in the room. Whenever possible, use the overhead projector or the chalkboard to show students what their papers should look like. After giving instructions, question the children and ask them to give examples so you can determine whether they understand what to do.

If you are giving directions for seatwork to several groups in preparation for reading group time, be sure the assignment for each group is clearly labeled. For primary grades especially, you might assign a color to each reading group. Then use that color chalk or ink to put asterisks beside assignments or worksheets taped to the board to indicate the appropriate group, or write the whole set of assignments and instructions in that color. Use the same location for each group's assignment everyday so they will know where to look without your reminder.

Standards for Form, Neatness, and Due Dates

You should develop a standard set of instructions for work requirements. Students will then learn what is generally expected, and you will only have to explain exceptions or changes to them as they occur. The will need to know such things as what paper to write on, what heading to use, whether or not to write on the back of the paper, whether or not to color any part of it, how to number, whether to use pen or pencil, and whether to erase errors or to draw lines through them.

Decide on a standard heading for students to use on their papers. Post a sample heading and go over it with students the first time they are to use it. Remind them of it several times during the early weeks of school until they use it properly. Make the heading as brief and simple as possible.

Finally, due dates should be reasonable and clear; exceptions should not be made without good cause. Be sure to tell students your policy for turning in work on time and follow it consistently. Don't keep extending time limits; if you do, children may learn to dawdle to avoid work. In general, insist that work not done on time be completed at home or after school. This assumes, of course, that students possess the necessary knowledge or skills to do the work.

Procedures for Absent Students

A number of problems arise when students are absent. They miss instruction, directions for assignments, and assistance they may need in getting work under-way. Establishing some routines for handling makeup work is helpful to these students and avoids interruption of class. Perhaps you will not require that students complete each assignment that they missed while they were absent, but a student who misses critical assignments will need to make these up. The following items should be considered:

1. Arrange to meet briefly with students who have been absent to point out what makeup work is required. If you post weekly assignment lists for each subject on a bulletin board or keep a folder with lists of assignments in an easily accessible place, you will be able to point out which of these are to be completed. For young children, you may need to have a packet of makeup work in a special "makeup folder." Be sure to let the students know how much time is allowed for makeup work.

2. Establish a regular time, such as fifteen minutes before or after school, when you will be available to assist students with instruction they have missed and makeup work. In addition, you can designate class helpers

who will be available at particular times of the day (usually during seat-work activities) to help these students.

3. Designate a place where students can turn in makeup work and where they can pick it up after it has been checked (for example, baskets or trays labeled "Absent In" and "Absent Out").

MONITORING PROGRESS ON AND COMPLETION OF ASSIGNMENTS

Monitoring Work In Progress

Monitoring student progress helps you detect students who are having diffi-culty and also enables you to encourage other students to keep working. Once you have made an assignment, you should give careful attention to student work. Don't immediately begin work at your desk or go to help an individual student without first checking to see if all students are starting work and are able to do the assignment. If you don't check, some students will not even start the assignment, and others may begin it incorrectly. Two simple strategies can help to avoid this situation. First, if everyone in the class is doing the same assignment you can assure a smooth transition into seatwork by beginning it as a whole-class activity; that is, have everyone get out paper, worksheet, or other materials and then answer the first question or two, or work the first few problems together as a group just as you would conduct a recitation. For example, ask the first question, solicit an answer, discuss it, and have students record it on their papers. Not only will this procedure ensure that all students begin working, but any immediate problems with the assignment can be solved. A second way to monitor student involvement in the assignment is to circulate around the room and check each student's progress periodically. This allows corrective feedback to be given when needed and helps keep students responsible for appropriate progress. Note the progress of all stu-dents, not just those who raise their hands for help. Check frequently with students who become easily confused or distracted. Another way to monitor work in pro-gress is to have students bring their work to you one at a time at some designated point in the activity. However, be careful to avoid having lines of waiting students.

If you are working with reading groups while some students are doing seatwork, don't wait until the end of the reading period to check student progress on seatwork. Go around to the students between meetings with reading groups to be sure the students are doing the work correctly.

Sometimes assignments are given that are not due for several days or even a week or longer. Examples include notebooks, reports, and science or social

Reprinted by permission: Tribune Media Services.

studies projects. When this is the case, you will need to be especially careful to monitor student progress. Define substages in the project or assignment and then set deadlines and goals for each of these parts. Collect and check work at each of these stages and give students feedback. This will help students organize their work and make it easier for you to monitor and evaluate their progress.

Monitoring the Completion of Assignments

Monitoring completion of assignments has several components. First, you will need to establish regular procedures for students to turn in completed work and for you to note whose papers have been turned in. Many different systems are possible. For example, you might have students put completed work in individual "mailboxes"; then you can determine at a glance whose boxes are filled and whose are lacking assigned papers. Or you might have students put completed papers on a certain corner of their desks so that they will be easy to spot and check as you move around the room. This procedure is especially appropriate when you do not intend to collect the papers. A third procedure is to have students turn in their work to different baskets for each subject. You must find time to check each basket frequently and record each completed assignment in your grade book. As an additional help you may also provide students with individual checklists to help them keep track of their own assignments.

You should also give some attention to how you are going to collect work. When all students will be turning in materials at the same time, the most efficient procedure is to have the work passed in a given direction until you have all papers in your hands. Materials such as workbooks that are inconvenient or bulky to pass might be collected by designated helpers and stacked in a particular spot. Papers or assignments that are turned in by students at varying times can be placed in appropriately labeled baskets, trays, or plastic containers. Avoid locating these drop-off spots in congested areas or where they might be distracting to nearby students. Be sure that students know the procedure you expect them to use. Following it consistently saves time and prevents confusion.

Maintaining Records of Student Work

An important part of your monitoring system is your record of student work completion. Generally these records will be a part of your grade book. You should organize the grade book so that you have a place for recording absent students each day; for example, by putting an *a* in the corner of the appropriate space. When setting up your grade book, you should set aside several lines per student and record grades and scores for each subject on a separate line, or you can use a different page for each major subject. If you record grades for different subjects on the same line, you will need a code such as different color pen or pencil to distinguish them. Or you can write in subject headings at the top of the page and separate them by heavy red vertical lines. If you have students from another teacher's class for instruction in a subject, be sure to leave space for those additional students on a page for that subject in your grade book. It will be your responsibility to supply the other teacher with report card evaluations, and it will be helpful to have all of the information in one place. Check with some experienced teachers at your grade level for suggestions on organizing your grade book.

You should record grades or other evaluations (E, S+, S, U) for major assignments and test results in your grade book. Whether to record an evaluation of other classwork such as worksheets or workbook pages is discretionary. This is not as common in the primary grades as in the intermediate grades, where more emphasis is placed on grading and a more complete record of daily work in major subjects is useful.

MANAGING THE PAPERWORK

Keeping up with all the papers can be overwhelming. One way to avoid mountains of "back papers" is to look over, grade, and/or record and return assignments quickly. Not only is this excellent feedback for your students, but it also helps you to spot students who are "fading" and to diagnose areas needing whole-class remediation. Another approach is to have students assist with checking assignments. While this must be supervised closely, the task should be well within students' capabilities. Also, be realistic about your grading capabilities. If you are behind in grading six sets of papers and are planning to assign essays due in two days, change your plans. Allow yourself enough grading time to do the job well—on the last paper as well as the first; try making a grading schedule to distribute a huge task into manageable segments, rather than plowing through until you are exhausted. Instead of collecting, checking, grading, and returning each assignment, try another routine: Go around the room and check each student's work yourself and give oral feedback. You can record a grade if you wish, at the same time. This type of checking is especially effective for written assignments that require holistic assessment. It is also fast, personal, and efficient.

Upper elementary or middle school teachers often find themselves departmentalized and expected to teach 100 to 150 students each day. To manage the paperwork involved in distributing, collecting, keeping up with, and returning papers, you must have an organized system. Two useful system components are color coding and using grade-book code numbers.

A separate color code for each class can simplify the process. For example, if first period is coded red, place a red plastic tab on that roll page in your gradebook, place papers to be distributed or returned to first period in a folder having a red label, clip papers collected with a red spring clip, and place a red dot in the corner of report cards of all first-period students.

Having students write their "grade-book code number" in the upper left corner of each paper helps you quickly alphabetize papers, spot missing papers, and record scores on the correct grade-book line. This number corresponds to the line number of the student's name and the period number: For example, 22/3 would indicate the student whose name is on line 22 in your third-period class. If you use this system, wait until the third week or so of school, when classes have jelled, before assigning numbers.

Distributing papers is made easier if they are counted out per class set beforehand. This often prevents your coming up one or two papers short and having to try to duplicate materials and teach class at the same time. It also enables you to place names of absent students on left-over papers, drop them in a coded file folder, and have them ready for those students when they return.

To collect papers some teachers use a separate basket labeled for each period and have students place papers in the appropriate basket at a designated time. Others have students pass papers up in a designated pattern, clip papers together with a color-coded clip, and place the papers in an "in" basket. If you plan to have students pass papers up, you can prevent "straggler" papers by describing, modeling, and practicing how it is to be done.

Returning papers is simplified if they are already filed together, labeled by period, and even possibly organized by rows. Homework and classwork papers may be distributed by students. Consider using weekly "assistant teachers."

FEEDBACK TO STUDENTS

Good monitoring procedures provide the basis for feedback to students. Frequent and regular feedback is more desirable than sporadic appraisal because it reduces the amount of time students spend making errors if their performance is incorrect. Appropriate times for feedback will occur as you monitor work in progress and after it is completed. Try to give students immediate and specific feedback: Tell them what they need to do to correct errors, then check their corrections.

Feedback about completed work cannot occur until after an assignment has been checked. Checking should be done within a day of work completion, so that students can benefit from the feedback and you will be able to keep track of their progress. If you find yourself bogged down with work to check, have your students help you. At most grade levels students can exchange papers or check their own work occasionally. Use student checkers only for assignments that they are capable of checking accurately, such as arithmetic worksheets or spelling quizzes that have specified right answers. Teach them a consistent system for marking right or wrong answers. Displaying correct answers with the overhead projector can make checking work in class proceed smoothly and accurately.

In the primary grades particularly, assignments are often short and easy to check quickly. Rather than collecting the work and checking it later, you can check each child's work as it is completed. If you have students bring their work to you, be careful to avoid the formation of long lines that distract others and waste time. Another method is to check work as you monitor each student's progress. If students have finished, have them place the completed work at a corner of their desks so that it is easy to see. This practice gives prompt feedback, cuts down on the amount of paper you must collect, and allows you to have students correct their errors much more quickly.

Pay careful attention at the beginning of the year to the completion of assignments. The first time a child fails to turn in an assignment without an apparent reason, talk with him or her about it. If the child needs help, provide it, but require the child to do the work. If the child neglects two assignments consecutively or begins a pattern of skipping occasional assignments, call the parent(s) or send a note home. Be friendly, be encouraging, but insist that the work be done. Don't wait until the grading period is over to note problems with assignment completion or assume that the report card grade will communicate this information effectively. The parent or parents can be the teacher's strongest ally in assuring that the child takes school work seriously. And you should not hesitate to contact parents. Most parents will appreciate your concern and provide you with support from home.

Reprinted by permission of King Features Syndicate.

Another procedure for communicating with parents is to have students take checked assignments home regularly. Be sure this includes good work and not just poor work. You can occasionally have parents sign and return the work as a way of rewarding and motivating students to "keep up the good work." Use a large envelope or a folder with two ends taped to convey the materials home rather than leaving them loose. This envelope or folder also is a convenient receptacle for other important documents the child must transport home for signing or for the parents' information. Be sure the child's name is on the folder or envelope. Taping a signature sheet on the front that has a place for the date and the number of papers included can ensure that parents see all the student's work.

Another means of giving the children feedback is to display good work. Note that you should not make standards for "good" so stringent that some children can never meet them. Effort may be a more appropriate criterion in some cases.

Finally, teach students how to keep a record of their own work. Older children can keep a sheet with test scores or assignment grades. Steps on a ladder or circles on a caterpillar to color in for each completed assignment, or some other similar visual device, can be a good motivator for younger students.

SUGGESTED ACTIVITIES

1. Case Studies 3-1 to 3-3 illustrate some effective accountability procedures that encourage student responsibility. Decide which ones you can incorporate into your classroom.

2. Case Study 3-4 illustrates problems that can occur if certain accountability procedures are not in place. Use the information in this and in previous chapters to diagnose Mr. Ambrose's problems. Compare your ideas with the keys in the Appendix.

3. Use Checklist 3 at the end of the chapter to organize your planning as you develop an accountability system. Can you think of any additional accountability procedures that you will need?

CASE STUDY 3-1

Procedures for Monitoring Student Progress. To help her students learn responsibility for their written work, Ms. Brown monitors student projects in class and promptly checks all papers. The first thing in the morning, she returns graded papers to students, who may then file correctly done work in their notebooks and correct all other papers before filing. Students with corrections to do are given help if necessary so they can complete them the same day.

When students work on written assignments in class, Ms. Brown circulates and systematically checks each student's progress. In addition, she has designated two class times for further progress checks. The first is in the fifteen minutes after returning from lunch, when Ms. Brown calls students up to her, one by one, to check their morning work while the rest of the class rests, takes turns using the bathroom, listens to a record, or reads library books. When assignments are incomplete, Ms. Brown discusses with the student how and when to finish. If the assignment can be checked quickly, Ms. Brown does so. For assignments too complex to grade quickly, she checks for completion and grades them later. Occasionally Ms. Brown uses this time to look over notebooks, checking for completeness and proper organization.

The second formal checking time is during the last few minutes of the school day. During afternoon quiet time while students listen to a story tape, Ms. Brown checks the papers in each student's mailbox against her daily work assignment check sheet. Under each subject category, she records the names of students who have not turned in that particular assignment. Before students leave school she calls the names of those from whom she has not received certain papers, saying, "I need a math [or spelling, handwriting, etc.] paper from these people." She posts on the chalkboard the names of students who have completed the day's assignments, and sometimes gives certificates of good performance to those who have worked especially well that day.

In addition to the two in-class checking periods, Ms. Brown uses spare moments to keep track of students as they are working. When time permits, she systematically walks around the room looking at each student's work, checking papers for correctness, and helping students with problems. She is careful to check frequently those students who are most likely to have difficulty with the work.

CASE STUDY 3-2

Keeping Students Involved During a Combined Reading Group And Seatwork Activity. Ms. Avery designates a section of the chalkboard for listing seatwork assignments during reading group instruction. A typical assignment consists of three parts: a reading assignment, workbook pages, and comprehension questions and activities. At the beginning of the reading period, Ms. Avery presents directions for any seatwork assignment that is common to all groups. She assigns the group she will meet with first a brief "get ready" activity to complete and bring to the reading circle. She then gives instructions to the other groups, one at a time, for their seatwork. Each group is told when they can expect to be called and how much progress they should make. She usually calls the low group up second to break up the long seatwork time for them. Before joining the first group, Ms. Avery quickly walks around the room to be sure each child has begun the seatwork assignment.

When she meets with each group (usually for fifteen to twenty minutes), she sits so she can see the entire class. She scans the class frequently and signals children when necessary to keep them on task. She does so by making eye contact or sometimes calling individuals' names softly to prevent or stop inappropriate behavior. Because Ms. Avery does not want students coming to her for help while she is in the reading circle, she has assigned one helper for each reading group. In order to prevent excessive use of the helpers, Ms. Avery has taught the children to request assistance only for situations that prevent them from doing any work at all. If they can skip the problem or question and proceed with the work, they are to do so and wait for help from her.

As soon as she dismisses a reading group to begin a seatwork assignment, she circulates around the room checking on student progress, answering questions, helping students, and making sure that students in the most recent group have started their assignment promptly. Between groups, checks usually take no longer than five minutes, after which she is ready to call the next group.

If her work with one reading group lasts more than twenty minutes, Ms. Avery plans a short task for them to do independently at some point so she can leave the group to circulate among the students doing seatwork. She reminds students of how much time they have left and encourages those who are lagging behind.

After meeting with all the reading groups, Ms. Avery tells students how much more time they have to complete their seatwork activities. During those minutes, Ms. Avery again circulates, helping and prompting students who are still working and checking the work of students who have finished. By the end of the reading instruction period she has checked everyone's work. If students have not completed one or more of the seatwork assignments, Ms. Avery notes this and talks with them about when they can finish their work during the day.

CASE STUDY 3-3

Math Accountability Procedures in an Intermediate Grade. In Mr. Wilson's fifth-grade class, math always follows the morning break. At the end of the break, Mr. Wilson displays four or five math review problems on the overhead projector screen and then rings a bell to signal the end of the break. At this point students work the warmup problems at their seats. Mr. Wilson sets a timer for five minutes and spends the time returning graded papers to students or taking care of other administrative matters. When math instruction begins, the warmup problems are checked along with the regular assignment.

Mr. Wilson stresses the importance of being organized, and he has students keep a math folder with sections. The first section includes an assignment sheet on which students copy daily assignments. The second page in that section includes several reminders for math, such as, "Always use pencil. Copy the whole problem unless told otherwise." Other sections of the notebook include warmups, class and homework assignments, and tests.

When checking work in class, Mr. Wilson usually reads the answers and has students place an X next to incorrectly done problems. After checking they write the number of correct answers at the top of the page and discuss any problems that have caused confusion. He then collects papers to check them himself.

Mr. Wilson takes special care during the math lesson to present new material slowly and clearly, to check students' understanding of the processes involved, and to allow ample time for classroom practice and questions. When students begin working on the classwork assignment, he walks around the room, systematically looking at each student's paper. He helps those who request it, and only after the first ten minutes or so of student seatwork does he sit down to look over the homework and warmup papers or to record grades. Students who need help while Mr. Wilson is at his desk raise their hands and are called up one at a time. If several students need help Mr. Wilson usually circulates around the class again.

The grading system is easily understood by students. The warmups for one grading period total one hundred problems, and the number of correct answers counts as one test grade. Classwork and homework grades make up 50 percent of the total math average and tests contribute the remaining 50 percent. In addition, Mr. Wilson provides bonus questions on tests, interesting problems, and math puzzles that students can complete for extra credit if they finish their work before the end of the math period.

CASE STUDY 3-4

Poor Work and Study Habits in a Fifth-Grade Class. Mr. Ambrose's fifth-grade class has been fairly well behaved and exhibits little disruptive behavior. Most students follow his procedures for procedural tasks, such as staying in their seats during whole-class presentations, raising hands during discussions, and using the pencil sharpener, restroom, and other areas of the room appropriately. Some social talk occurs during seatwork activities, but it does not escalate into chaos and students usually settle down when requests. However, students have been less task-oriented lately, and many students have been tardy turning in assignments. They complain that they don't know when assignments are due, and some don't turn in their work at all. In order to make assignments very explicit, Mr. Ambrose has begun to record the daily assignments on the side chalkboard. Because some assignments are not due until the following day, he leaves the previous day's assignments on that chalkboard also, so students will know when each subject's assignment is due for both days.

Today during a one-hour period of seat and group work, several students asked what they were supposed to do, in spite of the fact that Mr. Ambrose had listed the morning assignments on the chalkboard, and repeatedly pointed out where they could be found. After several students turned in papers before they were called for, Mr. Ambrose explained, "Remember that class assignments not finished during seatwork are supposed to be kept until the next day, even if you get them done later in the day, unless I call for them. If you finish the homework during seatwork time, it can be placed in the turn-in box then." Students continued to act confused, not only about when assignments were due, but also about how to do the work.

Mr. Ambrose frequently works at his desk during seatwork time, but he allows students to come up one at a time if they need assistance. They follow this procedure well, although some of the lowest achieving students seldom come up. Quite a bit of quiet socializing and other off-task activities go on among students whose seats are located away from the teacher.

Mr. Ambrose has ample activities for students. For example, during a recent one-hour segment of time, he gave students a seatwork assignment and then had them take a quiz (students were told to hold their seatwork papers until after the quiz was completed). Also an extra credit assignment was listed on the board for students who finished this regular work early. As he handed out the quiz and gave instructions, some students continued to work on the seatwork assignment. Later they had to go to Mr. Ambrose to find the instructions for the test, and several did not have enough time to complete the test. Mr. Ambrose has told students that they must work harder and do their best or their grades will suffer, but this seems to have had an impact only on the most motivated students in the class.

What steps could Mr. Ambrose take to improve the situation in his class?

✔ **CHECKLIST 3**

ACCOUNTABILITY PROCEDURES

Check When Complete	Area	Notes
	Communicating Assignments and Work Requirements	
☐	A. Where and how will you post assignments?	
☐	B. What will be your standards for form and neatness? —Pencil, color of pen —Type of paper —Heading —Due dates —Erasures	
☐	C. How will absent students know what assignments to make up?	
☐	D. What will be the consequences of late or incomplete work?	
	Monitoring Progress on and Completion of Assignments	
☐	A. What procedures will you use to monitor work in progress?	
☐	B. When and how will you monitor projects or longer assignments?	
☐	C. How will you determine whether students are completing assignments?	
☐	D. How will you collect completed assignments?	
☐	E. What records of student work will you retain?	
	Feedback	
☐	A. What are your school's grading policies and procedures?	

Check When Complete	Area	Notes
☐	B. What kinds of feedback will you provide, and when?	_____
☐	C. What will you do when a student stops doing assignments?	_____
☐	D. What procedure will you follow to send materials home to parents?	_____
☐	E. Where will you display student work?	_____
☐	F. What records, if any, of their own work will the students maintain?	_____
☐	G. How will you handle grading disputes?	_____

4

Getting Off to a Good Start

The beginning of school is an important time for classroom management because your students will learn behavior, attitudes, and work habits that will affect them the rest of the year. Of course, it is better if they start the year behaving appropriately rather than practicing sloppy work habits and misbehavior.

Your major goal for the beginning of the year is to obtain student cooperation in two key areas: following your rules and procedures and successfully completing all work assignments. Attaining this goal will make it possible for you to create a good environment for learning during the rest of the year.

A concern for establishing appropriate behavior does not imply a lack of concern for student feelings and attitudes. Instead, the intent is to create a classroom climate that helps children feel secure and that prevents problems from occurring. Therefore, some of the suggestions in this chapter will focus directly on cognitive goals, while others will incorporate student concerns and other affective considerations.

The major topics in this chapter are teaching your rules and procedures to the students, deciding on the classroom activities you will use during the first week of school, arranging these activities into workable lesson plans, and identifying needed materials. Finally, some special problems are discussed. A checklist is available to help organize your planning, and two case studies of the beginning of the year will give you many ideas about how to begin.

TEACHING RULES AND PROCEDURES

One of the surest ways to communicate your expectations for student behavior is through a planned system of classroom rules and procedures. How best to teach this system to your students is an important consideration. The term *teach* is used purposely; you will not communicate your expectations adequately if you only tell students about rules and procedures.

Three aspects of the teaching process are important:

1. **Describing and demonstrating the desired behavior.** Use words and actions to convey what behavior is acceptable or desirable. Be as specific as possible. For example, do not simply tell the children you expect them to be good while you are out of the room; tell them what "be good" means—stay in seats, no talking, keep working. You should demonstrate desired behavior whenever possible. For example, if you are going to allow "quiet talking" or "classroom voices" during seatwork, then you should provide demonstrations of what this means. If the procedure is complex, then present it in a step-by-step manner. For example, lining up requires that students know when to line up (e.g., the teacher gives permission by tables or rows), where and how to go (e.g., push chairs under tables and then walk without talking), expected behavior in line (e.g., hands off others, no talking in halls, walk—don't run). You do not need to do all the demonstrating; many students enjoy the privilege of showing the class the correct procedure.

2. **Rehearsal.** This means practicing the behaviors. Rehearsal serves two purposes: It helps children learn the appropriate behavior, and it provides you with an opportunity to determine whether the children understand and can correctly follow a procedure. Complex procedures may have to be rehearsed several times. Practice is especially helpful for primary-grade children; however, the older elementary school child can benefit from rehearsal whenever the procedures are complex or have not previously been encountered.

3. **Feedback.** After you have asked students to follow a procedure for the first time, be sure to tell them if they did it properly and then praise them. If improvement is needed, be sure to tell them that, too. Be discriminating in your feedback—for example, "I liked how quickly you put your materials away, but I did not like the talking by the students at Table Two." If many students do not follow a procedure correctly, then you should repeat one or more of the above steps. If only a few students are off track, you might ask them to describe what they are supposed to do, so that you can determine whether they understand your directions. Finally, the fact that students follow the procedure correctly once does not mean that they will do so consistently. You should watch them carefully and be prepared to give reminders and feedback as appropriate.

Two examples that illustrate how to teach procedures are presented below. The first example shows the teacher instructing students on the use of the correct heading on their papers. This procedure was taught to students on the first day of school in a fourth-grade class as part of an assignment to write a brief account of their summer.

Mr. Samuels has written a sample heading for students' papers on the front chalkboard. He points to it, explaining to students that he wants this heading to be on every assignment they do. He points to the upper right-hand corner of the sample page and explains that students should write the heading there. Mr. Samuels then tells students they should write both their first and last names on the first line. He points to the line below where he has written "Writing" and explains that this line is for the subject of the assignment and will change when students do an assignment in another subject. Students are then instructed to put the date with the month spelled out under the subject name. The teacher points out the room calendar and suggests that students refer to it when they need to know the date. Mr. Samuels then asks the class if there are any questions about the heading. When no questions are forthcoming, Mr. Samuels tells the students to take out a sheet of paper and pencil and to put the correct heading for a writing lesson on their paper. He then circulates around the room, checking to make sure that every student is using the proper heading.

Note that Mr. Samuels demonstrated the correct form by having an example on the chalkboard; he described each aspect carefully and gave students an immediate opportunity to practice the heading and to receive corrective feedback.

The next example shows how a complex transition procedure was taught to a second-grade class. The teacher in this example teaches students to respond to a signal, put away their materials, and move to a rug area.

Ms. Stevens explains to her students that she expects them to move quickly and quietly from one activity to another so that they will have time to do all the things that are planned. She shows them the kitchen timer and makes it ring. She tells the students that this will be a very important signal. When they hear this bell, the students should put away the materials they are using and move to the next activity as quickly as possible. "After reading I will ring the bell and then you are to put your reading materials in your desk as quickly as possible. You should then get up from your desk and walk carefully and quietly to the rug so that we can begin our Spanish lesson. Are there any questions?" A student asks if she will always ring the bell for Spanish and Ms. Stevens says she will.

Ms. Stevens then tells the class that she would like them to practice. "You have paper and pencil on your desk that you have been using to write a story. I will give you time to finish the story later in the day. Right now, when I ring the bell you should put your materials in your desk and come quickly and quietly to the rug." At this point Ms. Stevens rings the bell. Students immediately begin putting away their materials and moving toward the rug. However, several students line up to get drinks of water and one goes to the bathroom. When everyone is on the rug in a circle around Ms. Stevens, she refers to the clock on the wall and says, "It took us three minutes to put the materials away and get to the rug. You are second graders now, and I think you can move faster than that. I think you should be seated on the rug in a circle in one minute. Also, it was not time to get a drink of water or to use the bathroom unless it was an emergency. Do you all understand?" The students all nod solemnly.

Ms. Stevens then tells students to return to their desks, get out their paper and pencils, and get set to practice again. The students go quickly back to their desks and take out their materials. Ms. Stevens then rings the bell again, and students go through the routine, this time more quickly. After all the students are settled, Ms. Stevens smiles and thanks the students. "You've done a super job. It only took you one minute to get to the rug. I'm really proud of you."

In the example Ms. Stevens demonstrated the signal, described the desired behavior, and gave a rationale for it. The students were allowed to practice the process twice, and feedback was given to them each time.

PLANNING FOR A GOOD BEGINNING

You have already done a major portion of the planning for the beginning of the year if you have followed the guidelines in the first three chapters. Your room should be arranged, and you will have decided on your rules, procedures, and an accountability system. You now need to plan activities for the first several days of schools.

Important Considerations

For the first days of school you should plan activities that will allow all your students to be successful. Such activities will make students feel more secure and confident and encourage their continued good effort. Initial lesson and seatwork assignments should be easy and require only simple directions. In this way the children will quickly learn lesson routines and encounter little difficulty in completing assignments.

Plan activities with a whole-class focus. For the first few days you should limit the lessons to those that can be presented and explained to all the students at the same time. Do not try to group students for instruction for at least several days, and if you can, avoid individual testing or any activities or seatwork assignments that require you to work with individual students for long periods of time. Don't overload yourself or your students with unnecessarily complicated activities. Your students will already be learning many new procedures during the first few days of school. In addition, you will need to be free to watch students very carefully during the first few days in order to detect problems and take appropriate action. If you are involved with a small group or with an individual, you may not see important behaviors and events.

Plan your activities to take into account the children's perspectives, concerns, and needs for information about the new and unfamiliar situation that your classroom presents. A variety of activities, including some with physical movement and music, and provision for occasional short breaks will provide the changes of pace that help maintain interest and alertness throughout the day. In addition, you should stimulate the children's interest in the curriculum and associated activities. If you are excited about the wonderful things they will be learning this year, your students are more likely to feel that enthusiasm themselves. Foreshadow some of the interesting units in science and social studies, or tell them about some of the skills that they will develop in your class.

Some Typical Activities

Activities that you will use in the first school day and for several days thereafter are described below. They are not necessarily presented in the sequence you will use, nor will you use each one every day, so you should carefully examine the two case studies at the end of the chapter in order to see how different teachers put the pieces together.

Greeting the Students

Prepare student name tags ahead of time. Have extra materials on hand for unexpected students. Decide how name tags will be fastened. If you use straight pins you may be inviting little dueling matches and surprise pricks and pokes. If you intend to use safety pins, be sure your students can fasten them or plan to do it for them. Other options are tape, commercial stick-on tags, or a length of yarn to allow the name tags to be worn like a necklace. As well as using name tags, you might also tape a card onto the top of the student's desk and write the student's name on it.

When students enter the room, greet them warmly, help them get their name tags on, and get them seated. If you have taped their names to a desk, then the matter of seating is settled. In some cases, however, the roster of students is not definite, and you may not want to bother setting up a seating chart before the students arrive. In this case let the students choose their desks. (Make a seating chart and/or label desks with name tags as soon as practicable, making any necessary adjustments later.) Don't allow the students to wander around the room or to become noisy. If students straggle in and you cannot start class right away, provide a simple dittoed worksheet, a dot-to-dot drawing, or a picture to color so that students will have something to do at their desks. As soon as most students are present, begin with the introduction.

Introductions

You will want to tell the students something about yourself; however, an extended autobiography is not necessary. A few personal notes and something about your interests would be appropriate. Have students introduce themselves—nothing more than a name is necessary, but some teachers like to use a little more introduction, having the children tell something about themselves. The introduction activity should not take too long, however, as there will be plenty of opportunity later to get acquainted, and you do not want students to become restless.

Room Description

You will need to point out major areas of the room, particularly any areas that students will be using on the first day. As you do so, any procedures associated with room use that will be needed that day should be described to students. For example, show students where they may put their coats, lunches, or other items they bring from home; be sure they know where the pencil sharpener is and when they may use it, where frequently used supplies are stored, where the calendar, wastebasket, and clock are located, and so on.

Get-Acquainted Activities

Teachers frequently include a get-acquainted activity as part of their first day plan. Such activities can help children feel that the teacher and other children know them better and care about them as individuals. Teachers often describe the goal of such an activity as helping students feel more comfortable with their classmates and more secure. The activities are also used to foster a greater sense of class cohesiveness. One of the examples of get-acquainted activities described below can be used early in the first day's plan of activities. It will provide a nice change of pace after the room description or after the initial discussion of rules and major procedures.

- Ask students to introduce themselves and to name a favorite activity or hobby, or tell about something they did during the summer. Keep this activity moving briskly because student attention will wane during long introductions. A variation of this activity is to use reciprocal introductions. Have pairs of students learn each other's name and something about the other person (hobbies, interests). Then have each person introduce his or her partner.

- Use a name game to help students remember names and to add interest to introductions. For example, have students make up an adjective to go with their own name (e.g., Happy Holly, Curious Carl) or have students think of a food they like (Milk-Shake Marty, Pizza Pete). Then as students introduce themselves, have them name the other students who came before them (or perhaps the last five students) along with their adjectives or foods.

- Make ditto copies of a line drawing of the school's mascot. Then have each child sign his or her copy and write some personal facts (names of brothers or sisters, pets; likes and dislikes; favorite activities, foods, and so forth) on the drawing. Post these on a bulletin board so students can read about each other.

- Have students complete a brief questionnaire identifying their interests, favorite subjects, hobbies, etc. Upper elementary students can complete a series of open-ended statements that reflect their interests or preferences (e.g., "Today I feel . . ." or "The thing I do best is . . .").

The activities described below can be used the first day or later in the week, after students are more acquainted with one another or after you have time to prepare for the activity.

- Make a puzzle with student names. For example, leave out a few letters in each name for students to fill in. Or list first and last names in separate columns in scrambled order and let students match names, or students can identify names arranged in a "seek and find" puzzle.

- Set aside a few minutes before the children leave in order to review the day's activities and to discuss with the students what they learned, found difficult, liked best, and so forth. Say a few words about upcoming events and activities that the children will look forward to. Comment on good work and behavior to reinforce your expectations and to keep the tone positive.

- Have students from last year's class—you'll need to plan this well ahead— write letters to students in this year's class, telling them what to expect, what was fun about the year, suggestions for study, and what they learned during the year. Share these letters with your students.

- Have students bring a paper bag with three to five objects, such as books, pictures, or toys, that tell something about themselves. Let students use these props to introduce themselves on the second or third day of school. Split the activity into two segments if necessary to maintain attention and interest.

- Make up a questionnaire in the form of a scavenger hunt; for example, "Name a student who has three brothers and who plays kickball." Let students work in groups to see how many of their classmates they can identify.

- Have students bring in one item that represents them for a bulletin board. Each student will explain the meaning of his or her item to the class and put it on the bulletin board, forming a collage of student interests and experiences.

Presentation and Discussion of Rules, Procedures, and Consequences

Soon after the introductions, usually after the initial room description, you should present the major rules and procedures. School rules should be covered along with your classroom rules. Major consequences associated with the rules should be described at the same time. You should plan to review the rules later, perhaps on the second and third days, to confirm their importance and help students remember them. Posting the rules will serve as a reminder to students. You may have copies made of the rules and procedures and send these home for parent signatures. Important procedures should also be taught. Teach these procedures as they are needed, rather than all at once. For example, during this initial discussion you will probably want to teach procedures for using bathrooms and pencil sharpener, moving about the room, obtaining help, asking questions, and talking. Later in the day, as they are needed, teach other important procedures such as those for major transitions (ending the day, leaving and entering the room at lunch time, etc.) as well as procedures associated with recess, cafeteria, or other out-of-room areas. Your opening routine (see Chapter 2) will probably be used on the second day of school, so you may wish to wait until then to describe it to the students. Procedures for special equipment can wait until you're ready to use a particular piece of equipment, and small-group procedures should not be introduced until those activities are to begin. The idea is to provide students with the information they need to complete successfully the activities required of them in the first days of school and to help them feel confident in their new classroom environment.

On the second day of school you should review the rules and some of the major procedures students need to know. This reinforces your expectations for appropriate behavior and reminds students of rules and procedures they may have forgotten. When correcting students' behavior at the beginning of school, it is important to remind students of what rule was broken. In the primary grades particularly, you will need to observe students carefully for several weeks to be sure they are following procedures correctly and to give reminders, cues, and prompting to help them learn class routines.

When you present your class rules and procedures to students, set a positive tone by emphasizing the benefits to everyone: "These rules are intended to help us have an enjoyable class in which everyone can learn. We all know that our classroom will work better when everyone respects each other's rights," or "When we allow someone to speak without interrupting we are showing that we are good listeners." If some procedure or rule is difficult to follow, you might acknowledge this as you discuss it: "I know it isn't easy to remember to raise your hands before speaking when we are having an interesting discussion, but doing so will give everyone a chance to participate," or "It will be hard not to start using

Reprinted with special permission of King Features Syndicate.

"The hardest part about goin' back to school is learning how to whisper again."

the equipment right away, but we need to wait for directions so no one is injured." Explanations such as these help students understand and accept what might ordinarily be seen as arbitrary rules.

Content Activities

Be sure to select activities that are uncomplicated and that can be presented to the whole class. Seatwork assignments should allow for differences in speed of completion; be sure to have some backup activities for students who complete work early. Consult your teacher's manuals and curriculum guides and talk with experienced teachers to get ideas about appropriate beginning content activities for different subjects at your grade level.

Time Fillers

Periodically, you will need to fill in time between activities or before and after major transitions. For example, students may complete a seatwork assignment earlier then you anticipated, but there may not be enough time to begin another activity before the next scheduled event. Or there may be times when the students need a short break after an intensive lesson. Filling these times with constructive activity is better than trying to stretch out an already completed task or just letting students amuse themselves. Some ideas include having a good book to read to the children or some simple games that can be played in the classroom (such as Seven Up, Name Bingo, Hangman, Baseball Math, Spelling Bee). Keep on hand some dittos or other handouts with puzzles, riddles, or story starters for creative writing. You can also lead the children in group exercises, sing songs, listen to a good children's record, or have a bulletin board of creative writing ideas. Ask other teachers for ideas and accumulate a file so that you will be ready with a filler whenever one is needed.

Administrative Activities

You will need to distribute textbooks to students. You may wish to issue one or two textbooks on the first day; some teachers wait a day or two before distributing textbooks and use handouts and dittos for assignments, especially if class enrollment is likely to change. When you do give out books, you need to record book numbers for each student, perhaps using a standard form. You should also determine school policies in this area. For example, some schools require that books issued to students be kept covered at all times. If so, you will need a supply of covers on hand and you will need to be prepared to teach the children how to cover the books. In lower grades, it might be better to do the job yourself or enlist the help of parents or an aide. Even in higher grades, some students will have forgotten how to cover books. Plan to show the whole class, and schedule plenty of time for this event.

Determine whether there are any materials that students must take home with them on the first day or later in the week (this might include information about the breakfast and lunch program, school policy on attendance, time arrival and departure for children, etc.).

Communicating with Parents

It is a good idea to prepare a letter to send home to parents explaining any essential information that is not already conveyed via school handouts. Sometimes teachers at one grade level get together and collaborate on the letter. If not, write one of your own and get it ready to go home with the children at the end of the first day. Its purpose is to establish a link with parents and to communicate important information to them. The letter should include information on:

- Materials or supplies their child will need

- Your conference times and how parents may contact you

- Information on breakfast and lunch programs if not already provided by the school

- Special information you want them to know

   Special events for parents (e.g., back-to-school night, open house).

A cheerful, friendly letter that is neat, legible, grammatically correct, and free of misspellings will create a good impression and communicate a professional image to the parents. It is easy to get extremely rushed at the beginning of the year and to let this letter be slipshod. Have a friend proofread the letter before you duplicate it to be sure it is clear, correct, and easy to read. A handout describing class rules and major procedures (especially those relating to student assignments) might be sent as an enclosure with the letter. Having parents sign and return this handout will provide you with assurance that parents received your letter and enclosures.

Special Problems

While it is not possible to predict every problem that could occur in the first few days of school, it is possible to identify several that occur commonly, occa-

Glen Dines KAPPAN

"And then, of course, there's the possibility of being just the slightest bit too organized."

sionally, or rarely. If you are prepared for the commonly occurring problems and at least not surprised by the occasional or rare event, you will be able to cope.

Interruptions By Office Staff, Parents, Custodians, and Others (Common)

If you can manage the interruption without leaving the room, do so. Ask the interrupter into your room and face your children as you talk with the person. If the interruption is likely to last more than a few seconds or if you must leave the room, give the children something to do before continuing the conference. Let the interrupter wait, not your class. Ask your students to continue working if they are already involved in an activity. If not, tell them that they can use the time to read a book that they have at their desk or to rest their heads on their desks. It is a good idea to have materials for one or two planned activities ready for an unforeseen or lengthy interruption.

Late Arrivals on the First Day (Common)

Greet late arrivals as warmly as you did the other students. Tell them you will talk to them about what they missed as soon as you can, but that for now they must wait in their seats. Show them where to sit. When you have the total class involved in some seatwork activity, meet with these children to explain anything they may have missed.

One or More Children Are Assigned to Your Class After the First Day (Common)

Try to arrange to meet with these students before school so that you can explain rules and procedures to them and handle necessary paperwork. If you have already distributed books to the class, make sure these students also get texts. If you can't meet these students ahead of time, use the first available opportunity while the rest of your class is occupied with seatwork. Appoint one or more responsible students to be "buddies" with the new students to help familiarize them with the classroom and school procedures and rules. The amount of assistance you can expect from these buddies will depend on their grade level. Be sure to monitor new students carefully to help them adjust to your class and to learn appropriate behavior.

A Child Forgets Lunch Money or Supplies (Common)

Be familiar with your school's policies. The principal or school nurse may have an emergency fund for students without lunch money. Some schools allow students to charge a lunch in an emergency. It's a good idea to keep a couple of lunches' worth of small change on hand. Also, have one day's worth of supplies available for students who forget theirs. If a student continues to forget supplies, you may need to check with parents to see that they are aware that the materials are needed. If you suspect that the problem is that the family cannot afford the supplies, see if your school or parent-teacher organization has funds for helping such students.

The School or District Office Requires You to Complete Large Amounts of Paperwork During the First Week of School (Common)

Do as little of this during class time as possible. Plan to spend extra time before and after school and arrange your personal schedule to accommodate it. This will pay off in reduced tension over the long run. If you must do clerical work during class time, do it quickly while the children are engaged in seatwork activities. Monitor the class while you work and avoid losing eye contact with your students for long periods.

A Child Forgets His Bus Number or Misses Her Bus (Occasional)

Help to avoid these problems by rehearsing bus procedures with students (especially younger students). Have bus numbers and parents' and emergency phone numbers on hand for when these situations do arise. Make certain the child is not left alone while waiting for a ride, and reassure the child that you will not leave him or her.

Insufficient Numbers of Textbooks Are Available or Vital Equipment and Materials Are Missing (Occasional)

Before school begins, you should check on the availability of textbooks and your equipment and find out your school's procedures for getting the needed materials into your room. When you discover shortages, report them to the proper person from the school office. If you must begin the year without enough texts, you may be able to have students share books or you might arrange to share a class set with another teacher. If you have no texts at all in some subject, you can probably find earlier editions of the text in the book storage room to tide you over. Depending on the subject, dittos or other teacher-prepared materials may be sufficient.

One of Your Students Has a Handicap That Seriously Interferes With His or Her Ability to Understand You or To Follow Directions (Occasional)

Seat the child close to you and engage him or her in simple activities. Work individually with this student only after the rest of the class is busy. As soon as possible, talk to the child's resource teacher to determine what the child is capable of doing, then plan the child's educational program. If possible, talk to the child's teacher from the preceding year for suggestions. You will also find it helpful to set up a conference with the child's parents soon after the year has begun.

Crying (Occasional)

Younger children especially may tend to cry for no apparent reason early in the school year. The crying will usually stop fairly quickly if you can distract the child and engage him or her in some activity. Sometimes it helps to assign a friend to accompany the child to get a drink of water, wash his or her face, and then come back to join the class. Be understanding but do not reinforce crying by giving the child excessive attention or sympathy. If the crying is not disruptive, the child can remain in his or her seat until the episode is over. If the crying is disruptive, take the child out of the room or have someone from the office come to get him or her.

Wetting (Occasional)

While accidental wetting is more common with younger children, it sometimes occurs even in the upper grades, especially during the first few days of school. This kind of accident is extremely embarrassing to the child, and the teacher should make every effort not to add to the child's discomfort. Have some paper towels on hand to facilitate the cleanup and handle the matter as privately as possible. You should arrange to call home or have an office worker phone to bring a change of clothes to school. Later, talk privately with the child to determine why he or she did not go to the restroom in time. With some younger children, you may need to contact the parents and keep a change of clothes at school as a precaution. In general with younger children, the teacher needs to schedule regular bathroom breaks and even remind some children to use the bathroom regularly.

A Child Becomes Very Sick or Is Injured (Rare)

If the child has a known medical condition (such as epilepsy) and you have been previously informed of what to do, follow directions and stay calm. In other cases, phone the office or send a messenger requesting someone to come to get the child. Do not leave the child unattended.

SUGGESTED ACTIVITIES

1. Read the case studies at the end of the chapter and use these to help prepare your lesson plans for the beginning of school.

2. Use Checklist 4 at the end of the chapter to organize your planning activities for the beginning of school.

3. Talk with teachers who have had several years of experience at the grade level you will be teaching. Ask them what activities they use during the first few days and how they sequence them. Teachers are often willing to share handouts and ideas. You might also ask someone to look over your lesson plan for the first day and give you suggestions.

CASE STUDY 4-1

BEGINNING THE SCHOOL YEAR IN AN INTERMEDIATE GRADE
The First Day

Time	Activity	Description
8:00–8:04	Greeting students	Ms. Beech greets students individually as they enter the room, and she gives each a stick-on name tag. "Your desk has your name on it," she tells them, "and you may work on the puzzle page that is in your desk or you may wait quietly until I begin class." After the school bell rings, Ms. Beech greets a few latecomers and talks briefly with two parents while the children work on the puzzles. Then she addresses the class, telling them to put the puzzle page in their desks for now and that they will be able to work on it later. She waits while students put the puzzle sheet away.
8:04–8:09	Introductions	Ms. Beech then introduces herself and talks briefly about where she taught last year. She tells the class about the good things she has heard about them from their former teachers. She says that she has high expectations for this class. Then she asks each student to stand and say his or her name and tell where he or she went to school last year. Ms. Beech checks the roll at the same time.
8:09–8:16	Information about the class, etc.	Ms. Beech distributes letters that were written by her students from the previous year's class. Each letter is addressed to the new student who "inherits" the previous student's desk. The letter serves as an introduction to the teacher and the grade, describing what to expect during the year. Students read these letters eagerly, and there is a brief discussion of their contents.

Time	Activity	Description
8:16–8:22	Room introduction	The teacher briefly points out and describes procedures for some of the important features of the room, including storage shelves for supplies, drinking fountain, and bathroom facilities.
8:22–832	Discussion of rules and procedures	Then Ms. Beech explains some of the basic rules and procedures for the class, including her expectations that students will be kind to each other and raise their hands to participate in a class discussion. She explains when and how they are to sharpen their pencils, shows them the signal that she will use to get their attention, and tells them what they should do when they want her help during seatwork. During this discussion she stops frequently and checks to see if students understand. She asks several students to repeat or demonstrate the procedures for the class.
8:32–8:45	Get-acquainted game	She explains the directions for a get-acquainted game. A ditto is distributed that presents a list of challenges, similar to a scavenger hunt. During the activity students try to find other students who fit characteristics on the list—for example, "Find a student who is the same height as you are; has the same favorite television show; has the same shoe size; was born in the same month of the year; has freckles." Students are given ten minutes to work together, then the teacher leads a short class discussion.
8:45–8:55	Class discussion	Following this there is a class discussion in which the teacher solicits nominations for the name of a new school mascot. The students vote on the name they will submit.
8:55–8:59	Bus procedures	The teacher presents bus procedures. She asks students who ride each bus to stand, and she notes their names on a seating chart.

(Continued)

Time	Activity	Description
8:59–9:16	Language arts	She gives directions for a written activity that requires students to name things starting with different letters, for example, "a bird that starts with B," "a country that starts with U." She has students try one example before they begin. She checks to see if all understand. While they work she checks materials students have brought and writes their names on items.
9:16–9:26	Checking	The teacher leads a discussion and checking of the language arts activity. Students check their own work.
9:26–9:40	Book checkout	The teacher has students clear their desks except for a pen, and she passes out book covers and book cards. Students help distribute textbooks, one kind at a time. Students put their names in their books and they fill out a book card, using a model and information that the teacher displays on an overhead transparency. When they finish they look through their new books, and the teacher checks and takes up their book cards.
9:40–10:01	Covering books	Then the teacher demonstrates how to cover a book. She works in a small group with six students who did not raise their hand when she asked who knew how to cover a book without using tape or scissors. The other students cover their own books. The class works until all students have all three new books covered.
10:01–10:15	Discussion of school procedures	The teacher calls all the students to sit on the rug in a half circle. She sits facing them and goes over procedures for physical education (P.E.), hall passes, central office procedures, use of the phone, and bicycles on school grounds. She asks three students to explain the procedures in their own words.

Time	Activity	Description
10:15–10:30		Recess
10:30–10:35		Bathroom and water break.
10:35–10:47	Handwriting assessment	Students work on a handwriting sample, which will be used as a pretest for comparison with their handwriting at the end of the year. At the beginning of this activity the teacher demonstrates the heading form on the board and has all students head their papers. She then distributes a ditto containing a humorous poem, which students copy for their assignment. While students are working, Ms. Beech checks each student's heading.
10:47–11:20		Ms. Beech leads the class through a short review lesson in their new arithmetic book. The class does the first three problems together as a group. She assigns a practice problem, then circulates, looking at student work to see if all understand. Students do the remaining problems on their own.
11:20–11:27	Checking	After students have finished with their seatwork, the teacher uses this occasion to present to students the procedures that they will usually use to check work in class. The class checks the fifteen problems and then passes them forward to the teacher.
11:27–11:40	Preview of course content	The teacher surveys students about their favorite school subjects by asking for a show of hands: who likes spelling best, who likes arithmetic, and so on. She previews some activities in each major subject during the year and describes a field trip planned for the fall.
11:40–11:45		Ms. Beech has students put their materials away and prepare to leave for lunch. She describes cafeteria rules and she tells students that when they return to the room after lunch, they are to take their seats

(Continued)

Time	Activity	Description
		immediately. Then she will allow them time to use the bathroom and get ready for the afternoon. She reviews bathroom rules and has students repeat these.
11:45–12:15		Lunch
12:15–12:25		After lunch, Ms. Beech has students use bathroom, sink, and drinking fountain row by row. When not engaged in this activity, students may work on their puzzle pages or rest their heads on their desks.
12:25–12:40	Creative writing/ thinking	The teacher introduces a creative writing and thinking activity in which students generate lists of things that fit categories listed on a handout, for example, "Name things that are made of metal." She asks students to think of a few practice examples. The object is to think of as many different items as possible, particularly items that are not listed by anyone else in the class. Students work individually on this assignment.
12:40–1:15		Students leave the class to participate in one of their twice-a-week music classes.
1:15–1:30	Spelling pretest	Students return from music and students take a spelling pretest, which the teacher administers and collects.
1:30–2:00		The class checks and then discusses the creative writing assignment they completed before going to music. The teacher uses the discussion to introduce students to a science unit on metals and minerals, which they will begin later in the week.
2:00–2:23	Social studies	The teacher passes out a ditto with a paragraph that describes facts about the city in which the students live. She calls on several students to see if they understand the assignment, then circulates, checking to see if all students are successful.

Time	Activity	Description
		After reading the paragraph individually, students answer comprehension questions by filling in blanks on a ditto. The class then discusses these answers, while the students check their own work.
2:23–2:30	Getting ready to go home	Students prepare to leave for the day. Ms. Beech makes announcements, distributes some forms for students to take home, and reminds students what to bring with them the next day. She reminds bus riders about when and where they board their buses.

The Second Morning

Time	Activity	Description
8:00–8:08	Administrative routine	As individual students enter the room, Ms. Beech tells them to sharpen their pencils and head their papers, using the form that she has displayed on the chalkboard. While students do this, the teacher collects forms and lunch money and calls roll.
8:08–9:17	Discussion of rules and procedures	She then greets the class and reads them a newspaper clipping of a story about the first day of school. She leads a discussion of the news story, brings up similarities between the classes in the story and their own class, and discusses some common feelings about the beginning of school. She checks to see who remembers some of the school rules and procedures from the first day. She reviews these and discusses some problems that occurred yesterday after school. Ms. Beech gives the class some positive feedback about their behavior in class and reviews some class procedures and rules. She also discusses a new topic: what students are expected to do if they finish their work early. One option is

(Continued)

Time	Activity	Description
		free reading. She shows students where the magazine rack is and discusses use of the materials in it.
9:17–9:32	Language arts	The teacher reads some funny poems to the class. There is a brief discussion on one of the poems, led by the teacher.
9:32–10:15	Creative writing	The teacher introduces a creative writing exercise, using examples from the poems she read. Given a list of four unlikely pairs of objects, students must choose one pair and write a paragraph about how the two things are alike. Before students do this individually, the teacher presents one example and leads the class in listing similarities. Finally the teacher and class together make a list on the board of ways that things might be alike, then students work individually on their paragraphs while the teacher helps and encourages individual students.
10:15–10:30		Recess
10:30–10:35		Bathroom and water break
10:35–11:05	Review grammar lesson	Ms. Beech conducts a review grammar lesson. She asks students to stand if they know what a noun is, then she asks each standing student to name one noun. If the student makes an error, he or she must sit. Then the teacher solicits the definition of a noun and reviews with the class the three common categories of person, place, or thing. She introduces a new category (idea), giving examples and having students give examples.
11:05–11:25		Students work individually on grammar exercises on nouns in their new textbooks.
11:25–11:45	Checking language arts seatwork	The teacher leads the class in checking their grammar exercises. Students participate in discussing answers and checking the work.
11:45-		Lunch.

CASE STUDY 4-2

BEGINNING THE SCHOOL YEAR IN A PRIMARY GRADE
The First Day

Time	Activity	Description
8:00–8:10	Greeting students	Ms. Simpson greets the children as they enter, helps them put on their name tags, and checks the pronunciation of their names. She then instructs them to find the desk that has a laminated strip with their name on it. Ms. Simpson shows them where the crayons are and tells the children they may color a picture at their desks while they wait for everyone to arrive. She supervises the class as she waits for the last bus.
8:10–9:00	Introduction	When all students are in, Ms. Simpson introduces herself to the class, then instructs the students how to answer as she checks the roll. She tells the class that the first thing they are going to do is to get to know each other. She asks the students to stand, introduce themselves, and tell one thing that they like to do.
	Description of the room and bulletin boards	Following this, she discusses the various parts of the room and explains related procedures, such as when it is all right to use the restroom or pencil sharpener. After introducing and explaining each procedure, she has students practice it. She briefly describes some of the topics they will be studying, referring to a related bulletin board. Another bulletin board has a list of school supplies they will need and examples of each. After leading a brief discussion about how supplies will be used, Ms. Simpson tells the students she will have a list of supplies for them to take home that afternoon.
	Discussion of rules and procedures	The teacher discusses the rules that are posted: (1) we take turns; (2) we listen to others; (3) we wait quietly; (4) we walk where

(Continued)

Time	Activity	Description
		we want to go; (5) we respect others and their property. She encourages the students to offer the rationale and examples for each rule, and she praises them when they raise their hands to be called on.
9:00–9:15	Tour of school	Ms. Simpson then tells the students they are going to take a quick tour of the school. Before they line up, she explains the procedure they will use and her expectations for student behavior. She lets them practice lining up quickly and quietly. When students have returned to their seats after the tour, she gives them feedback on their behavior, noting both good points and things that need improvement.
9:15–9:45	Handwriting lesson	Ms. Simpson introduces a handwriting lesson. She goes over the instructions, being sure she has each student's attention. She asks two students to demonstrate the first parts of the lesson at the board. She passes out papers and sharpened pencils for students to use. She then has the class do a practice example using one letter. She checks to see that all understand. Students use the laminated strips on their desks to practice writing their names. After two lines of practice, students copy a riddle from the overhead transparency. Ms. Simpson moves around the room checking student work.
9:45–10:00	Story, review of hall rules	After the papers have been collected, Ms. Simpson discusses how to come up and sit on the rug and then has the students come up by tables. She discusses the answer to the riddle students copied, then reads a story. While she is reading, she shows pictures and asks questions about the content. Then she tells the students that they will soon be lining up to go to P.E. She has

Time	Activity	Description
		the students repeat the P.E. teacher's name and reviews the rules for walking down the hall.
10:00–10:30	P.E.	Students go to physical education.
10:00–10:35	Rest break, record	After the students return, Ms. Simpson puts on a record for students. She reviews restroom rules and then lets students use the restroom and get a drink of water, one table at a time.
10:35–11:15	Math	Ms. Simpson asks the students to take out the math books she has labeled with their names and place under each student's desk during P.E. She reminds students to use the sharpened pencil she gave them earlier. She holds up her copy of the book and explains that each day they will tear out a sheet to work on. She shows them how this is done and then has the students do it. She circulates, giving help when needed. Then she tells the students to write signs that they see in their neighborhoods. The teacher explains the purpose of the exercise and gives instructions. They do the first part of the assignment together; then students complete the assignment individually as the teacher circulates. Students who finish quickly are given a piece of drawing paper on which to draw a sign they have seen in their neighborhood.
		When all students are finished, they go over the answers orally. Ms. Simpson then gives instructions for the next worksheet in their book and has the students tear the page out. After doing a couple of problems together, she instructs students to finish this worksheet and then, one at a time, to bring both worksheets up to her so that she can

(Continued)

Time	Activity	Description
		check them. Again early finishers are instructed to work on their drawings.
11:15–11:30	Math summary and sharing	Ms. Simpson leads a brief summary discussion about the math assignment and then mentions other things they will be studying in math this year. She praises students for working quietly during math and asks if any students have a drawing they would like to show the class.
11:30–11:40	Discussion of lunch procedures	Ms. Simpson discusses the lunchroom rules and procedures and describes step-by-step what the students will do. She has the students go one at a time to use the restroom, wash their hands, and get their lunches if they have them. Then they line up and go to lunch.
11:40–12:10	Lunch	
12:10–12:25	Rest break	The teacher has the children put their heads down for a rest break, and she lets them use the restroom if they need to. While they are resting, the teacher plays quiet music on the record player.
12:25–12:55	Listening activity and English activity	Ms. Simpson passes out a dittoed worksheet for a brief listening activity. She explains that it is very important that students know how to listen well so that they will be able to hear information and instructions. She gives each student three crayons to be used in the activity period. Then she calls out what students are supposed to do; for example, "Circle a word starting with an M with the green crayon." She circulates among the students as she calls out instructions. After they are through, she appoints one person at each table to be that table's student helper and to collect the papers and hand them to her when she gets to the table. After she takes up this ditto she hands out another

Time	Activity	Description
12:55–1:15	Story introduction of booklet	Ms. Simpson calls the students to the rug by tables. When all students are seated, she compliments them on their behavior and reviews some of the rules. Then she reads a story to the students and leads a short discussion about it. Following this, the teacher describes a booklet they are going to be making this week, called "All about me." She describes each page that will be in the booklet and what should go on the cover. She gives each student the cover page of the booklet to illustrate and label and the first page, on which students are to draw themselves doing something they like to do. She shows them where to write their name on each page. Ms. Simpson says they can use their own crayons or borrow hers. They return to their seats as they get their papers.
1:15–2:00	Work on booklets	While students are working at their seats, Ms. Simpson walks around supervising their work, commenting on what a nice job they are doing. She writes children's names on materials they have brought from home.
2:00–2:10	Play break	She has the students place their papers in their desks and stand next to their chairs. She leads them in a few stretching activities and a quick game before she has a helper carry around a box to take up the crayons and pencils students used today.
2:10–2:25	Review of day's activities and rules	Ms. Simpson reviews the day's activities by asking, "If your mom or dad ask you what you did today, what would you tell them?" She also asks questions about the rules and procedures. She reminds the students to bring their supplies tomorrow and hands a dittoed list to each student. She tells those who have already brought supplies to leave

(Continued)

Time	Activity	Description
		them in their desks. They are also to leave their name tags in their desks for use tomorrow. She shows them how to put their chairs on the desks so they won't fall.
2:25–2:30	Getting ready to go home	Ms. Simpson reminds the students how to line up and calls the bus children to get in line first. She compliments the students on how well they put up their chairs, then leads them out of the room.

The Second Morning

Time	Activity	Description
8:00–8:07	Greeting students	Ms. Simpson greets the students at the door and asks them to place their supplies inside their desks, put on their name tags, and get a dittoed sheet from the front table to color.
8:07–8:20	Introducing beginning of class activities	When all the students are seated, Ms. Simpson explains the beginning of class activities they will be doing every day (pledge of allegiance, discuss the calendar, share thoughts). After having the students rise, she repeats the words to the pledge of allegiance, then has the students repeat it to her. Then she has the students move to the rug to sit in a circle. She appoints a student to add today's date to the calendar (on a bulletin board next to the rug) and name the month, day, and year. Ms. Simpson explains that when someone has a birthday, they will sing "Happy Birthday" at this time. Then she leads the students in a brief sharing time, allowing them to talk about favorite TV shows, what they like about summer, or other suitable topics after raising their hands to be called on.
8:20–8:35	Review of rules	Following this discussion, Ms. Simpson reviews the rules and some of the procedures

Time	Activity	Description
		presented yesterday, calling on students to state each rule and give examples of it.
8:35–8:45	Assigning helpers	Then Ms. Simpson describes each of the helpers she needs and their jobs and assigns jobs to volunteers, putting their names in slots on her helper poster.
8:45–8:50	Roll call	She asks the students to go back quietly to their seats and answer as she checks the roll. She reminds students to listen as she calls the roll so they will learn other children's names.
8:50–9:00	Administrative routine	She asks the students to take out one pencil. While they sharpen their pencils, one table at a time, she plays a record and allows students to sing along quietly. During this activity she passes out paper to be used in a diagnostic spelling test.
9:00–9:10	Diagnostic spelling test	When all pencils are sharpened, Ms. Simpson shows students how to head their papers, referring to a chart she has posted above the front chalkboard. Then she calls out the words for the test, giving a sentence using each one. After the test, she has students pass their papers to their table's student helper, who was appointed yesterday.
9:10–9:40	Handwriting and color recognition	Ms. Simpson has two appointed helpers pass out a sheet of handwriting paper and two dittos to each student. She instructs the students to copy twice (in pencil) the names of eight colors from the overhead projector, and then to complete the assignment, which calls for students to color appropriately a number of small animals on the ditto (black dog, purple fish, blue bird, etc.). When they finish they may get a sheet of drawing paper and color anything they would like.
9:40–9:55	Color recognition activity and story	Ms. Simpson instructs students to leave their papers in the upper left-hand corner of their desks for her to look at while they are at music, then she calls the students to the rug.

(Continued)

Time	Activity	Description
		She does a color word recognition activity with the students, then reads a story about colors and leads a brief discussion.
9:55–10:30	Reminder of hall rules and music	Before having students line up to go to music, Ms. Simpson tells students the name of the music teacher and reminds students of expected behavior in the halls and in music class. Students then are asked to line up by clothing colors to go to music. While the students are in music class the teacher checks the color papers and puts stickers on them.
10:30–10:35	Rest break	After the students return, Ms. Simpson puts on a record. Students are allowed to use the restroom and get a drink of water.
10:35–11:20	Math	Ms. Simpson tells the students to put their color papers in their desks and take out their math books and a pencil. She leads them through the first part of an activity, then has them work alone to complete the page. After going over the answers, she has the students do another page from the book, again starting the assignment together. Students who finish early are instructed to get a dittoed number puzzle from the front table to work on until everyone is finished.
11:20–11:35	Checking, math summary, puzzle	When everyone is finished, the second math page is checked by the whole class. Then Ms. Simpson discusses some of the concepts they have been using today and what they will be doing tomorrow. All students are given a copy of the puzzle and are told to work on it while getting ready to go to lunch. The puzzles will be checked tomorrow.
11:35–11:40	Review of rules	Ms. Simpson reviews the lunchroom rules and gives students feedback on their behavior so far today. She also mentions something about what they will be doing in the afternoon.

At the end of the second day of school all students received brief notes to take home to their parents. These notes were completed by the teacher while the students listened to a story record at the end of the day. Ms. Simpson called each student up to her, gave him or her the note and a hug. Attached to the notes were graded student papers from the first day of school.

During the following week, Ms. Simpson placed special emphasis on practicing student names, introducing and reviewing procedures as needed, practicing routines, encouraging student success, and consistently applying stated rules and consequences. She monitored students as they began to do independent work for longer periods of time. As students mastered basic procedures and were working more productively on their own, she slowly began to introduce interest centers and group work. The first few days served as a foundation on which to build more task variety into the school day. (Review Case Study 2-3, which describes a classroom that requires more complex procedures.)

✔ CHECKLIST 4

PREPARATION FOR THE BEGINNING OF SCHOOL

Check When Complete	Item	Notes
☐	1. Are your room and materials ready (see Chapter 1)?	_____
☐	2. Have you decided on your class procedures, rules, and associated consequences (see Chapters 2, 3, and 6)?	_____
☐	3. Are you familiar with the parts of the school that you and your students may use (cafeteria, office and office phone, halls, bathroom facilities, resource room, etc.) and any procedures for their use?	_____
☐	4. Do you have a complete class roster?	_____
☐	5. Do you have file information on your students, including information on reading and math achievement levels from previous	

Check When Complete	Item	Notes
	teachers, test results, and any other information?	_____
☐	6. Do you know if any of your students have handicapping conditions that should be accommodated in your room arrangement or in your instruction?	_____
☐	7. Do you have adequate numbers of textbooks, desks, and class materials?	_____
☐	8. Do you have the teacher's editions of your textbooks?	_____
☐	9. Do you know the procedure for the arrival and departure of students on the first day? For every day after that?	_____
☐	10. Are the children's name tags ready? Do you have some blank ones for unexpected children?	_____
☐	11. Do you have your first day's plan of activities ready?	_____
☐	12. Does your daily schedule accommodate special classes (e.g., physical education, music) or "pull-out" programs (e.g., Chapter 1 reading, resource room students, programs for the gifted)?	_____
☐	13. Do you have time-filler activities prepared?	_____
☐	14. Do you have a letter ready to send home to parents with information about needed school materials?	_____
☐	15. Do you know when and how you can obtain assistance from school staff members (e.g., the resource teacher, school nurse, librarian, office personnel, counselor)?	_____

5 | Planning and Conducting Instruction

Let's assume that the steps you have taken so far to ensure that your classroom will run smoothly have worked. Your classroom is organized, you've developed and taught your rules and procedures, and you have systems in place to manage student work. Now that your students are attentive and ready to participate, what do you do? Remember, your purpose is not to have a smoothly running classroom; your purpose is to help students learn. It is at this point that management and instruction meet. Well-planned lessons with a variety of developmentally appropriate activities support the positive learning environment that your careful management decisions have begun to create. Dry lessons with limited opportunities for student participation are boring and lose students; this is when management problems begin. Interesting well-planned lessons are the key to holding students' attention.

This chapter describes how to plan and conduct instruction in ways that support the kinds of learning you want for your students regardless of content area. Combining this information with information from your content area courses will help you teach each subject more effectively. The chapter is divided into three sections. The first part discusses the planning decisions you must make before you step into the classroom. The second section discusses how to implement those plans as you conduct instruction. The final section discusses some common problem areas such as transitions between activities and clarity of instruction.

PLANNING INSTRUCTIONAL ACTIVITIES

When teachers choose instructional activities for their classes, they consider several things. Primarily, they think about whether an activity will lead to student learning and what kind of learning they want to encourage. Activities that lead to better memorization are different from those teachers will choose to enhance reflective thinking or problem-solving. Next, teachers also must consider whether the activity will maintain student involvement. The sequence of activities in and the amounts of time spent on the various subjects in the curriculum must also be weighed. Such considerations lead many elementary teachers to plan reading and at least some language arts activities for the first two hours or so of the morning. These activities usually require sustained effort and often involve a combination of small-group and seatwork formats. Student involvement in these activities would be more difficult to maintain later in the day when students are less alert and more fatigued.

It is wise to establish a daily schedule with specific times allocated to different subjects. Doing so will help you remain conscious of time so that you do not shortchange subjects taught later in the day. Furthermore, students will be better able to pace their own work if they know what schedule will be followed. When you plan your schedule, try to arrange some change-of-pace activities to follow periods of sustained effort or intense concentration. For example, you might schedule recess, art, physical education, or music following the reading/language arts activities if possible. If you cannot schedule such activities conveniently, then at least give students a brief break and lead them in exercises, a song or two, or just give them a little time to stand and stretch.

When you begin to plan your daily schedule, you may find that your school district has established guidelines for the amounts of time to be allotted to different subjects. Also, special teachers may be assigned to teach a particular subject for certain days and times of the week. Thus you may find that your class will be taught physical education on Tuesday and Thursday from 1:30 to 2:00 and will have music on Monday and Wednesday from 10:30 to 11:00. Obviously your schedule will need to be set accordingly.

At the beginning of the school year, good planning requires extra effort. Overplanning—preparing more activities than can be accomplished in a particular time—and underplanning—preparing too little for the amount of time available—can occur, particularly with inexperienced teachers. It is better to overplan, then be flexible in implementing the plan. Activities not completed one day can serve as starters for second and third days.

Type of Plan

You will engage in several levels of planning, both long range (i.e., by the year and by the term) and short range (i.e., by the unit, the week, or the day). Each of these levels of planning should be coordinated. Accomplishing the longer plan requires dividing the work into terms, the terms into units, and the units into weeks and days.

The lesson outcomes you envision will determine your planning goals and objectives, and your plans should reflect these intended outcomes. Thus, your plans provide road maps that help transform the available curriculum into activities, assignments, and tasks for students. In developing your plans you should keep two important considerations in mind: first, what skills and concepts students must learn; and second, through which tasks and activities they can best learn them. The next section describes the tasks and activities that convey the content to students.

Types of Instructional Activities

For each subject that you teach, you will choose a series of activities to help students acquire skills or new learning, practice the skills, consolidate and extend their knowledge, and receive feedback about their learning. In this section the major types of instructional activities used to reach these goals are described. Then several concepts are discussed that are essential for the management of activities: sequencing, clarity, and activity flow.

Content Development

Although teachers sometimes present content to students individually or in small groups, whole-class presentation is often the major vehicle for introducing and teaching content activities. In our discussion we will assume that the content development activity is taking place in a whole-class format. During content development the teacher presents new information, elaborates on or extends a concept or principle, conducts a demonstration, shows how to perform a skill, or describes how to solve a problem. Whole-group content development activities are appropriate for learning goals such as exposure and familiarity and for the efficient presentation of factual material.

During content development the teacher takes an active role, focused on making students think about the new content, relate it to what they know, and apply it. One chief management concern is making sure that students are also active, not passive. Student involvement in the development of the lesson should be encouraged. Teacher questions are used for this purpose, allowing the teacher to check student understanding, to encourage students to contribute to steps in problem solving, to apply concepts or principles, or to analyze ideas being presented.

In addition to teacher presentations and questions, content development should include student activities such as sample problems or other demonstrations of understanding of the new content. These short activities not only help students learn the new content, but also provide the teacher with information about how well the class is understanding the lesson. Activities and teacher questions should be thoughtfully designed to expose students' thinking and understanding. For example, when a student gives a correct answer the teacher can probe with further questions like, "What led you to that answer?" "What do you mean by . . . ?" "What would come next?" Or "How else could you do that?" Other methods of checking for understanding are described in more detail in this chapter's section on achieving clarity.

Seatwork

In this activity students engage in assignments that provide practice or review of previously presented material. In the upper elementary grades, that portion of the seatwork assignment not completed in class often becomes a homework assignment unless the materials or resources needed to finish it are available only in the classroom. (Procedures for seatwork have been discussed in Chapter 2.)

Seatwork is useful mainly for consolidating or applying prior learning through practice rather than for learning new content. For that reason and also because it is difficult to maintain student involvement in lengthy seatwork activities, periods of student seatwork should be moderate in length whenever possible. When the seatwork period is likely to be long (e.g., more than twenty minutes), you should provide some variety. If students must engage in seatwork for a long period, as they are often expected to do when you are working with other students in small groups, give two or three short assignments on different topics rather than one very long assignment. One method of breaking up long seatwork assignments for those students with shorter attention spans is to have them do their group work with you second rather than first or last. This allows them to work independently for fifteen to twenty minutes, then shift to a teacher-supervised small group, and finally move to independent seatwork or learning centers for the next fifteen to twenty minutes.

A form of seatwork, which we will call classwork, is often used in conjunction with content development activities and before giving students a more extensive

"You mean we have to process all that data?"

seatwork assignment. In classwork activities the teacher selects a small number of exercises, problems, or questions that review the material presented during content development and preview the seatwork assignment. Students are asked to complete the exercises individually; then the teacher has students check and review the work as a whole class or group. This enables the teacher to check immediately for student understanding and ability to do the assignment and to provide quick feedback or reteaching if necessary.

Checking

In this activity students check their own seatwork or homework. The activity is appropriate only when the judgment of correctness can easily be made. Checking provides quick feedback to students, and it allows the teacher to identify and discuss common errors on assignments. Careful monitoring during checking is important to be sure that students are doing it correctly. Students must be taught to check papers accurately, so it is important for you to explain the procedures as well as model them and allow students opportunities to practice. When student checking is used, you should collect the students' papers and examine them, even when you record grades in class, in order to keep abreast of student progress and problems.

Recitation

This activity is a question-and-answer sequence in which the teacher asks questions, usually of a factual nature, and accepts, guides, or corrects student responses. The sequence of question/answer/evaluation is repeated frequently, with many students being asked to respond until a body of content has been covered. In effect, a recitation is a form of checking that is done orally. It can be used as a skill drill or to review student understanding of a previous lesson or assigned reading. It can also be used to check spelling, knowledge of vocabulary words, or other factual recall.

When recitation is used to check student understanding, it is important to distribute questions to all students, not just to those who are eager to answer. Calling on only those who volunteer can give you an inaccurate impression of the class's understanding. Develop a way to check systematically who gets a turn to answer. This can be done by using a checklist or a shuffled stack of name cards. It is helpful to ask the question, allow time for students to think, and then call on individual students. Limit the time you call on only those students who volunteer. Sometimes teachers use choral or whole-group responses as a way of keeping everyone alert and active. These kinds of responses are usually helpful only at the beginning of concept development as new material is being introduced and practiced. Sometimes teachers do not allow students enough time to respond, thus reducing opportunities for students who are slow to answer. Some experts recommend a "wait time" of several seconds—e.g., three seconds—before giving a prompt or calling on another student.

Discussion

Discussion is used to encourage students to evaluate events, topics, or results; to clarify the basis for their opinions; to help them become aware of other points of view; or to help them improve their oral expression skills. Sometimes discussions are begun with a recitation activity in which the facts of the content to be discussed are reviewed. Compared to a recitation, however, discussion questions are more likely to elicit the students' judgments, impressions, ideas, and opinions; also, teachers are less likely to evaluate the student responses directly. Instead, students are encouraged to express themselves, to examine their opinions and beliefs, and to understand other perspectives. Students may respond to each other rather than only to the teacher. The teacher's role then becomes one of encouraging, clarifying, and using student ideas, rather than evaluating their correctness.

When using a discussion format, careful planning of questions is needed. Students also should be made aware of your ground rules for participation (for example, raise hands, listen carefully, respect each person's right to speak). You must model, and students should practice, the procedures for participating in class discussion. Discussion activities are difficult to sustain in the primary grades for very long; even in intermediate grades, discussion should be limited to very short times (about ten minutes) until you have an idea of what you and your students can handle.

Student Work in Groups

This activity should not be confused with small-group instruction, which is described next. During student work in groups, two or more students work together on a task that requires their cooperation. This activity might be used for drilling on new vocabulary words or spelling, working on a science or social studies activity, discussion or problem-solving, reviewing for a test, preparing a group report, or building a display or other art project. Small groups work best when goals are clear and the steps to achieving them are understood by the students.

Small groups should be carefully monitored to be sure they are on track and to provide appropriate assistance. One way to help discussion groups stay on track is to assign a specific role to each member and have each group responsible for reporting back to the class. Tasks could include a reader/monitor responsible for reading and clarifying the task to the group and rereading as necessary if the group gets off the subject, a turn maker responsible for seeing that all group members have equal input into the group discussion, a pacer responsible for managing the time so that all parts of the task are completed, a recorder responsible for taking notes, and a reporter responsible for presenting the result of the group's efforts to the class. Other types of group-based tasks, such as science labs, might have somewhat different role assignments.

When assigning and managing group work, do not assume that your students possess the necessary skills for working together effectively. Instead, plan to teach them how to listen to others, take turns, summarize, reach concensus, etc. Such skills should be explained or demonstrated prior to beginning group activities and reviewed when necessary.

Small-Group Instruction

In this activity the teacher works with small groups of students, one group at a time, while the rest of the class works independently. This mode of instruction is most commonly used for reading and is frequently used for mathematics instruction as well. Its purpose, of course, is to accommodate a wide range of achievement levels in basic skill subjects. Because small-group instruction is used so extensively for basic skills, we will describe its features in detail.

A critical aspect of small-group instruction is that at least two different activities occur simultaneously. A teacher leads a group while students outside the group participate in a variety of independent activities. Because the teacher is actively involved with the small group, it is more difficult for him or her to monitor the behavior of other students and give them assistance. And because students may work independently for a long period, very careful planning and extra effort are required to keep them involved in their work.

The first step in setting up effective small-group instruction is to set the stage for the out-of-group activities. Give directions to the whole class at once, including the following: instructions for each assignment; a description of materials that will be needed; and, to help students pace their work, a suggested time for completing each activity. This list of assignments should also be posted or written on the chalkboard. Check whether students understand the directions by asking students in each group to review them before beginning.

Before calling the first group, monitor the beginning of independent work for a short time. After you are certain that students have started, signal the first group. During your work with the small group, monitor out-of-group students by scanning the room frequently. If you observe inappropriate behavior that is interfering with work, try to stop it with eye contact or some nonverbal signal, by calling the student's name once, or by reminding the wayward worker of what he or she should be doing. A "time-out" desk near you can also be used for a student who persists in misbehavior: You can signal such a student to go to the desk for a while, without your having to leave the group.

Another problem to consider is how students needing help on an independent task can obtain it without interrupting the teacher. Some teachers tell students to skip work they cannot do and go on to another activity until the teacher is available to assist them. Others allow students to help each other, or they assign a few students (perhaps one for each table or group) the role of helper. This works best if students are seated in mixed-ability groups. Finally, students can sign up on the chalkboard or on a clipboard sheet to indicate the need for assistance when you are available. If you must leave the small group to help a student or to deal with a problem, be sure to give students in the group something to do. One student in the group may be able to lead the activity for a short time.

When work with one small group has been completed, the next group should not be called immediately. Instead, take the opportunity to check the progress of the students who will be continuing individual assignments and help them with any problems they have encountered. Briefly inspect all students' work, whether or not they have requested assistance. Students who were off-task while you were teaching the small group can also be given delayed feedback at this time. Be sure to encourage and give positive feedback to students who are participating appropriately. The students who have left the small group and are moving to other activities should also be monitored to be sure they begin their activity promptly. Then signal the next group to come for instruction.

Arranging Activities within a Lesson

In any given subject, lessons usually consist of a series of activities. A common activity sequence in basic skill areas is:

1. Checking or recitation
2. Content development
3. Classwork
4. Seatwork, group work, or discussion

The first activity allows the previous day's assignment or homework to be corrected. If there was no homework, the teacher leads a review of prior content important for the day's lesson. During content development, new content or skills are taught. Following this, a short classwork activity is used to review the new content and to preview the new assignment. Then practice is provided through the seatwork, group work, or discussion.

The problem with that sequence is that it requires that the presentation of lesson content and the practice period each be handled in two, usually lengthy, segments. A variation of the sequence that accommodates more complex content and that does not demand as much sustained student attention is:

1. Checking or recitation
2. Content development
3. Classwork or seatwork, usually brief, with checking
4. Content development
5. Classwork, usually brief
6. Seatwork, group work, or discussion

This sequence allows the teacher to divide the lesson content into two parts, with practice and feedback following the first content development activity. Teaching new content in two parts with an intervening practice period will help students consolidate learning from the first part before they are asked to contend with the new learning required in the second part. The sequence also allows the teacher to check student understanding and to provide prompt feedback before moving on to more complex content. Furthermore, when individual activities are divided into shorter segments, student attention is usually easier to maintain. A problem with the sequence is that it produces more transition points and thus greater potential for student disengagement. Usually these transitions can be managed without difficulty, however, because student movement, new materials, or drastically changed lesson focus will not be required in the content development-classwork-seatwork cycle. Thus, the various activities will blend together, usually without conspicuous transitions.

Of course, not all lessons will fit either of the activity patterns described above. For instance, a science or social studies lesson may consist of a relatively long period of active student exploration or problem-solving in small groups followed by a whole-class content development discussion. Ongoing projects may entail long segments of individual seatwork or small-group work interspersed with short segments of whole-class or small-group instruction. Nevertheless, the two common patterns described above provide useful frameworks for building most lessons.

Planning for Clear Instruction

Once you have an idea of the range and sequence of activities that are available to you, you need to examine the content, concepts, and goals of the lessons and units that you will be teaching. One way to start is to review the unit and lesson in the teacher's edition of your textbook(s). Pay careful attention to suggestions for lesson development and activities. Study the exercises, questions, problems, and other activities in the textbook and decide which items would provide appropriate review of lesson objectives. Note examples, demonstrations, and key questions and activities to use in the development of the main concepts. Try to anticipate problems students may encounter in the lesson or assignments. Check for new terms and be ready to define them and present examples. Do some of the classwork or homework assignment yourself to uncover hurdles students will face. You can then build some helpful hints into your lesson or give extra emphasis to these difficult areas. If some items in the seatwork assignment go beyond the lesson scope, do not assign them as classwork or homework until you can teach the necessary content. If the content is not essential and you do not plan to teach it later, then assign such items only as enrichment or extra-credit activities.

Consider the interest the lesson is likely to have for students. Will you be enthusiastic about teaching this material to your class in this way? Your enthusiasm about the lesson is contagious and signals to students how you feel about its

Reprinted by permission: Tribune Media Services.

importance. If you find it interesting and exciting and you communicate this excitement to your class, students will probably respond with interest. However, if you find yourself unenthusiastic about a lesson or topic, chances are that your students will share your feelings. Consider approaching the lesson in a different way. For example, rather than giving a lecture presentation of material, perhaps you can find ways for students to contribute through large-group or small-group discussions that address the same issues.

Finally, organize your lesson parts into a coherent sequence. If the lesson is complex, write down or outline the main components. Then you will be well prepared for a clear lesson presentation.

Presenting New Content

If students understand where a lesson is going, they are more likely to be there with you at the end. Tell students what the lesson objectives are, either at the beginning of the activity or during it. If the lesson is at all complex, give students an outline to help them follow its organization. An outline helps organize the content for the students and provides a road map to keep them on course.

If students are to understand content from silent reading or from viewing a film or filmstrip, provide a content outline with a few items filled in and spaces for students to supply the rest. This task focuses attention and provides motivation for careful reading or watching. Go over these items with the class after the film, especially if the students use the outline for further work or study.

As you present a lesson, stay with the planned sequence unless an obvious change is needed. Avoid needless digressions, interruptions, or tangential information. Inserting irrelevant information into a lesson only confuses students about what they are expected to learn. Displaying key concepts, new terms, major points, and other critical information on the overhead transparency screen or the chalkboard will underscore their importance.

Presentations should be as focused and concrete as possible. Use examples, illustrations, demonstrations, physical props, charts, and any other means of providing substance and dimension to abstractions in the lesson. Avoid the vague expressions and verbal time fillers that, at best, communicate little information and make presentations difficult to follow. Allow students time and opportunity to process the information you're presenting.

Checking for Understanding

Find out whether students understand a presentation during the lesson; do not wait until the next day. As content development activities unfold, ask students questions to verify their comprehension of main points. You can also ask students to provide a written response to key questions and then check some or all of the students' answers either orally or by examining the written work. Asking students to demonstrate comprehension at several points during a presentation not only allows you to verify their progress, but also keeps students more involved in the lesson.

You can also check student understanding and emphasize main points by conducting an oral recitation after a presentation. Do this by asking a series of questions that recapitulate the lesson sequence and its major concepts. Be sure to involve many students in answering these questions so that you can identify the overall level of understanding in the class and reteach what has not been satisfactorily learned.

Other methods of checking for understanding include having students respond to your questions by the following:

- Displaying the correct one of two or more possible answers by holding up prepared color-coded cards.

- Using designated body movement (i.e., thumbs up or thumbs down, arms crossed or arms uncrossed).

- Folding a piece of notebook paper into fourths, using each of the eight sections to write responses, and holding them up for you to see.

- Writing in their own words explanations of the concept studied and turning these in for your inspection.

- Pairing with a designated neighbor and quietly explaining a concept or process to the other while you circulate and listen.

- Writing a question about the concept studied to ask a partner (any that cannot be answered are turned in for whole-class explanation).

- Keeping a journal or a learning log that includes entries on each lesson in a particular unit.

KOUNIN'S CONCEPTS FOR MANAGING GROUP INSTRUCTION

A central theme in managing activities well is the idea of activity flow. This means the degree to which a lesson proceeds smoothly without digressions, diversions, or interruptions. Lessons with good flow keep student attention and are less likely to offer opportunities for deviation because most of the cues for student behavior during the lesson will be directed toward behaviors appropriate for the lesson. When lesson flow is jerky, with frequent interruptions and side trips, there is more competition for student attention from cues external to the focus of the lesson. Therefore, there will be a greater tendency for students to go off-task.

A series of classroom research studies by Kounin and his colleagues (Kounin, 1970; Kounin and Gump, 1974) identified several concepts that contribute to effective management of interactive group activities, leading to smooth activity flow.

According to Kounin, activity flow is maintained through three types of teacher behaviors: preventing misbehavior, managing movement, and maintaining group focus. Within each class of behavior there are two or three related concepts. Let us look at how each is defined and consider some examples. These concepts are summarized in Table 5-1.

Preventing Misbehavior

Classrooms are complex settings. Many events can occur at the same time. One cannot always predict with certainty what will occur when. New teachers run the risk of focusing too closely on single events or on select areas of the classroom and missing the big picture. Understanding of two of Kounin's (1970) concepts, withitness and overlapping, helps to prevent this mistake.

Withitness is the degree to which the teacher corrects misbehavior before it intensifies or spreads to more students and also targets the correct student when doing so. A teacher who is not "with it" either will fail to stop the problem until it has escalated and may require a major intervention, or else will fail to catch the perpetrator and instead target either the wrong student or a Johnny-come-lately to the scene of the crime. It is apparent that underlying aspects of withitness include good monitoring and prompt handling of inappropriate behavior, concepts that will be discussed in detail in Chapter 6.

Overlapping refers to how the teacher handles two or more simultaneous events: for example, a visitor comes to the door in the middle of a lesson; a child from out of the group comes up to the teacher during reading group time; several

Calvin and Hobbes
by Bill Watterson

CALVIN & HOBBES © 1989 Watterson. Dist. by UNIVERSAL PRESS SYNDICATE. Reprinted with permission. All rights reserved.

TABLE 5-1 How Effective Managers Maintain Activity Flow (Kounin, 1970)

Issue	Skills	Definition	Example
Preventing misbehavior	Withitness	Communicating general awareness of the classroom to students; identifying and correcting misbehavior promptly and correctly	The teacher makes eye contact with a student who is about to "shoot a basket" with a wad of paper. The student puts the paper away. A student behind him, who has seen the interaction, decides he's not likely to get away with shooting a basket either.
	Overlapping	Attending to two or more simultaneous events	The teacher is leading a class discussion when a student comes in late. The teacher nods to him, continuing the discussion. Later, when students have begun a seatwork assignment, she checks in with him and signs his tardy slip.
Managing movement	Momentum	Keeping lessons moving briskly; planning carefully to avoid slowdowns	The teacher notices that explanation of a relatively minor concept is taking too long and distracting attention from the primary focus of the lesson. The teacher makes a mental note to go more in depth on this concept in a separate lesson the next day, and moves on.

Issue	Skills	Definition	Example
	Smoothness	Staying on-track with the lesson; avoiding digressions and divergences that can lead to confusion	While being responsive to student interests, the teacher avoids comments that tend to draw attention away from the key points of the lesson.
Maintaining group focus	Group alerting	Engaging the attention of the whole class while individuals are responding	Each student has a number that was drawn from a hat on the way into class. The teacher draws numbers and uses them to call on students during a fast-paced review.
	Encouraging accountability	Communicating to students that their participation will be observed and evaluated	At the end of discussion and practice of a new skill, students are told to turn to a neighbor and explain the process to him or her.
	High participation formats	Using lessons that define behavior of students when they are not directly answering a teacher's question	While some students work problems at the board, students at their desks are instructed to check them by working the problems on paper.

students get into a squabble while the teacher is busy helping other children across the room. A teacher who has good overlapping skills will handle both events in some way, instead of dropping one event to handle the other or else ignoring the second event. To handle an interruption, for example, a teacher might tell the class or group to continue working, or to get out some work, and then deal with the interrupter. The squabble taking place away from the teacher might be handled by eye contact or a brief verbal desist while the teacher stays with the students.

Notice that a teacher who is with it and exhibits good overlapping skills is able to insulate lessons from the intrusions that student misbehavior or external interruptions might cause. Furthermore, by reacting promptly to problems (but not overreacting) the teacher will often be able to use simple measures (eye contact, redirection, a quiet desist) that will not interfere with ongoing activities or distract students very much. If a teacher is not with it or does not overlap when needed, then lessons may be interrupted by student misbehavior and by the teacher's subsequently more visible and tardy reactions.

Managing Movement

Whereas withitness and overlapping are accomplished by handling external interruptions and student intrusions into the flow of the lesson, movement management is accomplished by avoiding teacher-caused intrusions or delays. Good movement management is achieved through momentum and smoothness.

Momentum refers to pacing and is indicated by lessons that move along briskly. Teachers can cause slowdowns in momentum by dwelling on individual parts of a lesson, direction, or skill and by unnecessarily breaking an activity into too many parts. For example, teachers should provide a standard heading for assignments that can be used routinely, rather than altering its form and having to explain it over and over.

Smoothness, as opposed to jerkiness, is epitomized in lesson continuity. A smoothly flowing lesson keeps student attention, while one that jumps from hither to yon distracts. Kounin used graphic labels to depict ways that a teacher might diverge from a smooth lesson. He described these divergences as "flip-flops," "dangles," "thrusts," and "stimulus-boundness." These problems are compared in Table 5-2.

Maintaining Group Focus

Classroom instruction involves teaching children in groups, often a whole class at a time. Doing so means that a teacher needs to be conscious of the group influence on the instruction. Like a conductor leading an orchestra, the teacher must elicit the performance of the individuals and still provide signals and direction to the whole class. Group focus can be maintained through several techniques.

Group alerting means taking action to engage the attention of the whole class while individuals are responding. It can take the form of creating suspense, telling students they might be called on next, calling on students randomly, asking students not reciting to listen carefully because they might be called on to add to the answer, or by using some new visual aid, display, or attention-getting

TABLE 5-2 Common Problems in Maintaining Momentum and Smoothness (Kounin, 1970)

Problem	Definition	Example
Dangle	Teacher leaves a topic or activity "dangling" to do something else or to insert some new material.	"All right, please take out your math books. Turn to page . . . Oops, I forgot to send this form to the office. Raise your hand if you ride the bus. All right, where were we?"
Flip-Flop	Like a dangle, except that the topic inserted is left over from an earlier activity.	"OK, let's leave vocabulary now. We'll pick up the discussion tomorrow. Please move your chairs into your writing groups. Take your pencils and a blank piece of paper, and that's all." (Students move into their groups and the teacher begins to give instructions for today's writing activity.) "All right now, does everyone understand what I want you to do? Oh, and did everyone remember to write down their vocabulary workbook assignment? I put it on the board, pages 235–242. OK, go ahead and start."
Thrust	Teacher inserts some information at a point where students are involved in another activity, and it seems irrelevant to them.	Students are working quietly on a standardized test. The teacher has been circulating and offering help; otherwise, there is scarcely a sound in the room. The teacher looks up and comments quietly, "When you're done, bring your test booklets to the front table and put your answer sheets in this box." Students continue to work quietly. When they begin completing their tests, the teacher must explain to each one individually where to put the test booklet and answer sheet.

(Continued)

TABLE 5-2 *(Continued)*

Problem	Definition	Example
Stimulus-bound	Teacher is distracted by some outside stimulus and draws the class's attention to it and away from the lesson.	Students are taking turns reading their writing aloud. Each student's reading is followed by comments from the rest of the class. During one such discussion, the teacher notices a student reading a paperback. "What are you reading, Alice?" she asks. "Have you read anything else by that writer?"

strategy. In contrast, poor group alerting would be engaging in a dialogue with one student or calling on students before asking questions.

Accountability occurs when the teacher lets students know that their performance will be observed and evaluated in some manner. It does not require a letter grade or a score (although it might), just communicating some degree of awareness of how students are performing. For example, the teacher might ask everyone who knows an answer to raise a hand and then call on one or more of those students; or the teacher could have all students write down answers and circulate to check them. The teacher might also have students keep notebooks and check them from time to time.

High participation formats are lessons that program the behavior of students when they are not directly involved in answering a teacher question. Such lessons have a higher built-in rate of participation than do lessons that merely assume that students will sit and watch when other students respond. Higher participation formats occur when students are expected to write answers, solve problems, read along, manipulate materials, or perform some other concurrent task.

Some activities lend themselves more to one type of group focus than another. When planning instruction it will be helpful to consider which of the three aspects to use. For example, during a demonstration that involves expensive materials, it might be difficult to use a high participation format, but group alerting might be easy to incorporate.

Kounin's concepts for managing group instruction not only help identify key aspects of effective teaching, but they can also be used to diagnose instructional problems and identify possible solutions. For example, if lessons seem to drag and student response is unenthusiastic, there may be a problem with group focus; a solution may be to work on alerting or accountability or to increase the degree of participation. Activities that take too long and that seem to get off-track constantly might have a problem with movement management. Perhaps the teacher should check for slowdowns and jerkiness.

TROUBLESHOOTING COMMON PROBLEMS IN CONDUCTING INSTRUCTION

Two areas give many teachers difficulty in conducting instruction: transitions and clarity. This section focuses on some common problems in these areas and suggests possible solutions.

Transitions

The interval between any two activities is a transition. Several management problems can occur during transitions, including long delays before starting the next activity and high levels of inappropriate or disruptive behavior. Transition problems can be caused by a lack of readiness by the teacher or the students for the next activity, unclear student expectations about appropriate behavior during transitions, and faulty procedures for transitions. Following are some examples of transition problems along with some suggested ways of correcting them.

Transition Problem	*Suggested Solution*
Students talk loudly at the beginning of the day. The teacher is interrupted while checking attendance, and the start of content activities is delayed.	Establish a beginning-of-day routine, and clearly state your expectations for student behavior at the beginning of the day.
Students talk too much during transitions, especially after a seatwork assignment has been given but before they have begun working on it. Many students do not start their seatwork activity for several minutes.	Be sure students know what the assignment is. Post it where they can easily see it. Work as whole class on the first several seatwork exercises so that all students begin the lesson successfully and at the same time. Watch what students do during the transition and urge them along when needed.

Transition Problem

Students who go for supplemental instruction stop work early and leave the room noisily while the rest of the class is working. When these students return to the room, they disturb others as they come in and take their seats. They interrupt others by asking for directions and assignments.

Suggested Solution

Have a designated signal that tells these students when they are to get ready to leave, such as a special time on the clock. Have them practice leaving and returning to the room quietly. Reward appropriate behavior. Leave special instructions for what they are to do when they return either in a folder, on the chalkboard, or on a special sheet at their desks. Or for younger students, establish a special place and activity (e.g., the reading rug) for returning students to wait until you can give them personal attention.

During the last afternoon activity students quit working well before the end; they then begin playing around and leave the room in a mess.

Establish an end-of-day routine so that students continue their work until the teacher gives a signal to begin preparations to leave; then instruct students to help straighten up the room.

Whenever the teacher attempts to move the students from one activity into another, a number of students don't make the transition, but continue working on the preceding activity. This delays the start of the next activity or results in confusion.

Give students a few minutes' notice before an activity is scheduled to end. At the end of the activity students should put all the materials from it away and get out any needed materials for the next activity. Monitor the transition to make sure that all students complete it; do not start the next activity until students are ready.

As the teacher gives directions during a transition, many students do not pay attention and continue to work, put their materials away, or get out new materials.

Don't try to give instructions during a transition except to individual students. Instead, give the whole class instructions before the transition begins. Don't begin explaining the new activity or presenting content until everyone is ready and listening.

Transition Problem

A few students always seem to be slowpokes during transitions, delaying the rest of the class.

Suggested Solution

Don't hold up the rest of the class for one or two students. Go ahead and start, but be sure to monitor the dawdlers in later transitions to find out why they are having trouble. Then give them individual feedback and close supervision.

The teacher delays the beginning of activities to look for materials, finish attendance reporting, pass back or collect papers, or chat with individual students while the rest of the class waits.

Have materials organized ahead of time, and once transitions begin, avoid doing anything that interferes with your ability to monitor and direct students.

The preceding items summarize the major problems that occur in classrooms at and around transition times. If you feel that your class is wasting time or if you are having difficulty keeping control during transitions, then a look at the suggested solutions may prove helpful.

Clarity

Communicating information and directions in a clear, comprehensible manner is a very important teaching skill. Clear instruction helps students learn faster and more successfully; it also helps students understand your directions and expectations for behavior more readily. Although clarity is important in all classroom activities, it is crucial during content development when nearly all new subject matter is introduced and taught. This section will focus on ways to improve clarity during this critical portion of your lessons.

Clear instruction results from several factors: the organization of information into a coherent sequence, use of an adequate number of illustrations or examples, precision and concreteness of expression, keeping in touch with student comprehension, and providing enough practice to ensure mastery. The following chart illustrates some of the many ways teachers can be both clear and unclear in their instruction.

Poor Clarity

1. Communicating Lesson Objectives
Not describing the lesson's purpose or what students are expected to learn

Being Clear

Stating goals or major objectives
Telling students what they will be accountable for knowing or doing

Poor Clarity	Being Clear
Not calling students' attention to main points, ideas, or concepts	Emphasizing major ideas Reviewing key points or objectives at the end of the lesson

2. Presenting Information Systematically

Presenting information out of sequence, skipping important points, or backtracking	Outlining the lesson sequence and sticking to it
Inserting extraneous information, comments, or trivia into the lesson	Sticking to the topic, holding back on complexities until the main idea is developed
Moving from one topic to another without warning	Summarizing previous points, clearly delineating major transitions between ideas or topics
Presenting too much complex information at once or giving directions too quickly	Breaking complex content into manageable portions, giving step-by-step directions, and checking for understanding before proceeding

3. Being Specific

Presenting concepts without concrete examples	Providing a variety of illustrations
Using overly complex vocabulary	Using words students understand; defining new vocabulary terms
Overusing negative phrases (e.g., not all insects, not many people, not very happy)	Being specific and direct (e.g., the beetles, one-third of the people, discouraged)
Being ambiguous or indefinite: maybe, perhaps, sort of correct, more or less right, you know	Referring to the concrete object precisely, stating what is and is not correct and why.

4. Checking for Understanding

Assuming that everyone understands, or simply asking, "Does everyone understand?"	Asking specific questions or obtaining work samples to be sure students are ready to move on
Moving to the next topic because time is short or no students ask questions	Asking students to summarize main points to verify comprehension Reteaching unclear points

Poor Clarity	*Being Clear*
Not calling on slower students, relying only on feedback from a few volunteers	Checking everyone's understanding

5. *Providing for Practice and Feedback*

Not assigning classwork or homework	Being sure students have adequate practice so that critical objectives are mastered
Giving assignments that cover only a portion of the content	Reviewing assignments to be sure that all of the lesson's skills are reinforced
Not checking, reviewing, or discussing students' assigned work	Checking work regularly, reexplaining needed concepts, reteaching when appropriate

SUGGESTED ACTIVITIES

1. Use Checklist 5 at the end of the chapter to plan one or more lessons.

2. Read Problems 5-1 through 5-3, which describe problems three teachers are experiencing with the management of instruction. After reading each paragraph, review this chapter and decide what strategies they might use to help overcome their problems (other chapters may also provide useful suggestions). You might use each problem as a basis for a group discussion and generate a list of many possible solutions or strategies. Then compare your list with the keys in the Appendix.

3. See how many examples of Kounin's concepts you can find in Problem 5-4. Compare your list with the keys in the Appendix.

4. Case Study 5-1 illustrates problems that can arise in conducting instruction. Use the concepts in this and in previous chapters to diagnose Ms. Lake's problems. Compare your list with the keys in the Appendix.

PROBLEM 5-1

Ms. Kendall is beginning her first year of teaching fourth graders. She is writing out her plans for the first few days of class. She has familiarized herself with the scope and sequence of the fourth-grade curriculum. One of the first decisions she will make is about her class schedule. She must decide how best to organize her students' day.

What should she consider as she develops her daily schedule?

What long-term plans should she make to ensure that students learn to manage their own academic work and develop good work skills?

 PROBLEM 5-2

During reading instruction Mr. Hart generally works with a small group of students while the remaining students do assigned work. Lately Mr. Hart has noticed that some students are not following seatwork directions and never finish their work, although he feels he allows appropriate amounts of time for work to be completed and gives thorough instructions before the reading groups start. A few students finish early, turn in their papers, and then wander around, interrupting other students and socializing excessively. Mr. Hart has to stop his work with the group in order to quiet the students. What can Mr. Hart do to get students to work more productively during seatwork?

PROBLEM 5-3

Ms. Jackson is trying to include more science lessons in her curriculum. She wants to try a discovery approach with her third graders. For a lesson on how sound is made, Ms. Jackson passes out paper cups in two sizes to students. Her plan is to have them hum into the cups and feel the different vibrations. However, as soon as students receive their cups, they begin to plop them noisily on the desks. Some students poke holes in the bottoms with pencils. Other students place them over their ears and show their neighbors, while another group is trying to figure out how to make the cups stay on their heads as hats. Ms. Jackson cannot get their attention back to the lesson. How could advance planning have helped her to avoid these problems? Use Checklist 5 to help you analyze this lesson.

 PROBLEM 5-4

As he is about to begin class after lunch, Mr. Case makes eye contact with two students who are exchanging notes; the students quickly get out their class materials. "Let's begin by working some of the exercises at the end of the chapter; you will need a piece of paper with a heading." As students begin to get out their materials, Mr. Case calls out, "Oops! I forgot to tell you to bring money for tomorrow for the field trip. How many of you will be going?" After a brief discussion, students finish getting out their materials. Mr. Case says, "We'll go through these exercises orally, but I also want you to write the answers on your papers as part of today's classwork. I'll come around later and check your answers. Now who can answer the first question? Hands please. Tyrone?"

Mr. Case conducts the lesson by calling on various students, some with hands up, others seemingly at random from the nonvolunteers. About halfway through the exercises, a student enters the room and says that he is new to the school and has been assigned to the class. Mr. Case goes to his desk, sits down, and says, "Okay, come here. I'll check out some of your books to you. I wish the school office wouldn't send children in the middle of the day. Where are you from, anyway? That's a nice shirt you are wearing."

After finishing with the student and sending him to a seat, Mr. Case leaves his desk and says to the class, "Now where were we? Oh, yes, question 7. Say, where did Kim and Lee go? I didn't give them permission to leave."

After several more minutes, Mr. Case calls a halt to the activity and says, "Now I'd like us to discuss the test coming up this Thursday. Let's make sure that you are all clear on what will be on the exam and what you will need to get ready for it." After a pause, he adds, "I almost forgot. Get your questions from before and look at the next to the last one. We need to add an important point that was left out. . . ." After finishing the item, Mr. Case turns the topic back to the upcoming test: "Now, where were we? Oh, yes. I need to show you some items that will be similar to those on the test. Here's one." He writes it on the chalkboard, then pauses: "Well, I don't want to give away the test, do I?"

Without discussing the test further, he turns to another topic: "Just wait until you hear about the video tape we will be viewing tomorrow. I borrowed it from another teacher, and she said that her students thought it was one of the most interesting, exciting stories they had ever seen!"

CASE STUDY 5-1

A Science Lesson in a Sixth-Grade Class. Ms. Lake has been having great difficulty obtaining acceptable or even completed work from many of her sixth-grade students. They never seem to be able to follow instructions or directions, even for assignments in the textbook. Only the most able four or five pupils are actually doing good-quality work. Ms. Lake likes to challenge the students with new ideas in order to stimulate their curiosity and promote independent thinking.

While much of the class appears to enjoy her presentations, the students just don't seem to be able to transfer their enthusiasm to their assignments. For example, in a recent science assignment students were supposed to draw pictures illustrating stages in the evolution of birds from reptiles; most students did not perform satisfactorily. The lesson preceding this assignment included the following components: a five-item test covered questions on birds, reptiles, and vertebrates, reviewing some content covered during the preceding week. Students checked their own answers to this test in class and then passed them in. Although it was not a difficult test, most students got three or fewer items correct. After the checking activity, the teacher began a twenty-minute presentation on the possible evolution of birds from reptiles. The following topics were discussed:

- The meaning of adaptation, with an example supplied by students.

- An example of environmental action in the local community. This topic was introduced by a student, and other students added comments.

- The possibility of life on other planets, including a discussion of the number of solar systems in our galaxy.

- A consideration of the question of why birds might evolve from reptiles, with a student's answer, "To get away from enemies, they would take to the air," as the only reason given.

- The classification system of living organisms: kingdom, phylum, class, order, genus, and species.

At this point in the presentation students were instructed to copy the classification system from the board. Ms. Lake also provided an example of classification, using the lion in the animal kingdom, vertebrate phylum, mammal class, etc. Two similar examples were also presented and listed on the board. The teacher asked if students understood and if they had any questions. No questions were forthcoming, so the teacher gave the assignment of illustrating the stages in the evolution of a reptile to a bird. Students were given twenty-five minutes and told, "Use some color in your picture, make it neat, and use three stages." As was the case with many of the assignments Ms. Lake gave, only a few students completed their work satisfactorily, although most seemed to make an effort to do some drawing, and many students checked frequently with Ms. Lake to see if their pictures were acceptable.

What problems are evident and what changes might Ms. Lake make to achieve more success in helping students complete assignments satisfactorily?

✔ CHECKLIST 5

PLANNING FOR INSTRUCTION

Check When Complete	Before the Lesson Ask Yourself	Notes
☐	1. What are the most important concepts or skills to be learned?	
☐	2. What kind of learning is your goal (memorization, application)?	
☐	3. Are there difficult words or concepts that need extra explanation?	
☐	4. How will you help students make connections to previous learning?	
☐	5. What activities will you plan to create interest in the lesson?	
☐	6. What materials will be needed? Will students need to learn how to use them?	
☐	7. What procedures will students need to know to complete the activities?	
☐	8. How much time will you allocate for the lesson? For different parts of the lesson?	
☐	9. If activities require students to work together, how will groups be formed? How will you encourage productive work in groups?	
☐	10. What examples and questioning strategies will you use? Prepare a list of examples for explanations and list higher order questions.	
☐	11. How will you tell during and after the lesson what students understand?	
☐	12. What presentation alternatives are there if students have trouble with concepts? Peer explanation, media, etc.?	
☐	13. Are there extra- or special-help students?	

Check When Complete	Before the Lesson Ask Yourself	Notes
☐	14. How will you make sure that all students participate?	_____
☐	15. How will you adjust the lesson if time is too short or long?	_____
☐	16. What kind of product, if any, will you expect from students at the end of the lesson?	_____
☐	17. What will students do when they finish?	_____
☐	18. How will you evaluate students' work and give them feedback?	_____
☐	19. How will the concepts you present be used by students in future lessons?	_____

6 | Maintaining Appropriate Student Behavior

As you have seen in the first five chapters, good classroom management depends on very careful planning of the classroom's organization, rules, procedures, initial activities and instruction. All of this planning and preparation will pay large dividends once the students arrive. However, being ready is not sufficient to sustain good behavior throughout the year. You will need to be actively involved in maintaining student cooperation and compliance with necessary classroom rules and procedures. You cannot assume that students will behave appropriately just because you carefully taught them what was expected of them. In primary grades, children are in the early stages of learning "going to school" skills, so constant attention to prompting good behavior will be needed. Even in the intermediate grades children need teachers who encourage good behavior by using their rules, procedures, and consequences consistently.

In particular, you should not be lulled into complacency by the good behavior of your students at the beginning of the year. Most elementary classes are quiet and subdued on the first day or two of school. Without careful teacher attention to maintaining good behavior, even a class that seems to begin very well may ultimately become disruptive and difficult to control. The following brief example illustrates such a class and also suggests some of the reasons why management problems might develop.

Ms. White carefully discussed her classroom rules and procedures with her fifth-grade class at various times on the first several class days, and students were generally well behaved. However, at the start of the third week problems are beginning to occur. While making presentations to the class, Ms. White stands at the front chalkboard in order to jot down important points. When she turns away from students to write on the board, students at the back of the room begin talking quietly among themselves. Some pass notes, throw paper wads, and leave their seats during seatwork assignments. If Ms. White reprimands students for talking, they say that they do not understand what to do and that they are just seeking help from each other. If she allows students to help each other during seatwork, before long everyone is talking, few are working, and the noise level becomes very high.

At first, students raised their hands for permission to speak. Later some students called out comments, and rather than ignore the contributions, Ms. White began to accept them when they were substantive. Now more and more students have become loud and distracting. Because discussion activities do not seem to work very well, Ms. White has begun to reduce the amount of time spent on these activities and to assign more seatwork.

During reading instruction, Ms. White meets with students in small groups while the rest of the class works on individual assignments. While working with the small group, Ms. White is interrupted more and more frequently by seatwork students who are having problems with the assignments. At other times she has to interrupt small-group instruction to deal with misbehavior outside the group. At the end of the small-group instruction period for reading, Ms. White frequently is dismayed to see what little progress students have made on their seatwork assignments.

Problems such as those that are occurring in Ms. White's class often have a gradual onset, developing over several weeks or even months. It is usually possible to avoid these problems, but to do so you must first understand why the problems occur and what you can do to prevent them. Because they develop gradually, the causes are not always apparent to the teacher or even to an observer unfamiliar with the history of the classroom. However, the capsule account of events in Ms. White's class suggests several reasons why things are beginning to go awry. One source of problems is that Ms. White is not monitoring student behavior carefully enough. Talking, inattention, and misbehavior are going undetected until the noise or commotion level is high. In addition, Ms. White is not checking student progress on assignments frequently enough. This reduces student accountability and prevents the teacher from providing the assistance that students may need to achieve the learning objectives.

A second problem is that Ms. White is being inconsistent in her use of procedures and in her reaction to students when they do not follow the procedures. By accepting some call-outs and by allowing noisy talk during seatwork, she invites students to continue to test the limits until the procedures finally break down.

A third problem, related to the first two, is that too many inappropriate behaviors are being ignored. As a result, students are unsure of behavior standards, and minor events are escalating into major disruptions involving substantial numbers of students. Finally, the teacher's attention is becoming more and more directed at inappropriate behavior, and no attention or incentives for appropriate behavior are evident.

These problems can be prevented or handled by the following four important guidelines:

- Monitor student behavior and academic progress carefully.

- Be consistent in the use of procedures, rules, and consequences.

- Deal with inappropriate behavior promptly.

- Build a positive climate with an emphasis on reinforcing appropriate behavior.

The remainder of the chapter considers how these guidelines can be implemented.

MONITORING STUDENT BEHAVIOR

To monitor classroom behavior effectively, first you must know what to look for. Two categories of student behavior are especially important to monitor:

1. Student involvement in learning activities.

2. Student compliance with classroom rules and procedures.

Student involvement is indicated by many behaviors, including attention during presentations and discussions and satisfactory progress in seatwork and other assignments. Students' compliance with classroom rules and procedures will be easy to monitor if you have a clear set of expectations for student behavior and have communicated these to the class.

Reprinted by permission: Tribune Media Services.

Monitoring student behavior during presentations requires that you stand or sit so that you can see all the faces of the students, and that you scan the room frequently. Some teachers are not effective monitors of student behavior during whole-class activities because they focus their attention on a limited number of students (usually those seated in the middle rows or tables and at the front desks); other teachers "talk to the chalkboard." In either case the teacher does not have a very clear perception of overall student response to the presentation, nor is he or she fully aware of what may be occurring at the periphery of the classroom. During your presentations, therefore, try to move around and develop "active eyes." If you notice a commotion involving several students and you have no idea of what is going on, this is a sign that you have not been monitoring closely enough.

When instructing a small group of students while the remainder of the class is engaged in individual seatwork, be sure to sit where you have an unobstructed view of all the students. Don't become so absorbed in working with the small group that you lose track of the other students. Look up frequently and be alert for problems. After finishing with one group, circulate around the room and provide needed assistance before calling the next small group.

When students are working on individual assignments and you are not instructing a group, you should monitor the class by moving around the class-room and checking each student's progress periodically. You will of course help students who request assistance; however, you should not just "chase hands" or you will not be aware of the progress of other students. It is very difficult to monitor student progress on assignments from your desk or from any other fixed location, so spend as little time in one place as possible. If you must work at your desk for a time, get up periodically and circulate around the room, looking at each student's work. If you must spend a long time (more than a minute or two) helping an individual student, avoid doing it at the student's desk unless you can monitor the rest of the class from that position. If the student's seat is in the middle of the room, for instance, half of the class will be behind you. In such a case call the student to a small-group work table, to your desk, or to some other location from which you can easily see all the students. Finally, when you work at your desk or at any other location, don't let students congregate around the area. They will obstruct your view of the class, and they will probably distract students seated nearby. Instead, call students to you one at a time.

A monitoring technique that is effective in getting students started on their seatwork is to begin the work as a whole-group activity. That is, have students get out the necessary materials (be sure to look for these on the students' desks), head their papers, and then do the first exercise, problem, or question under your direction. Then check and discuss the first item as a group. Using this approach, you can easily scan the room to be sure that everyone has begun and check on whether students understand what to do.

A critical monitoring task is checking assignments. Collect them regularly and look them over, even when students check their own work in class. Keep your grade book current so you will be able to detect students who skip assignments. If you teach an intermediate-grade class, you may sometimes give a long-term assignment. If so, be sure to check progress regularly. You may even give a grade or assign points toward a grade at these points. In upper elementary grades you may also have students keep a checklist of assignments and due dates.

CONSISTENCY

The dictum "be consistent" has been repeated more frequently than the pledge of allegiance. It is still worth some discussion, though, because its meaning is not always clear. In the classroom consistency means retaining the same expectations for appropriate behavior in an activity at all times and for all students. For example, if students are expected to work silently during seatwork activities on Monday, the same procedure is in effect on Tuesday, Wednesday, and the rest of the week. Penalties should also be applied consistently. For example, if the penalty for missing assignments is losing one's place on an honor list, the teacher must make sure that all students who skip assignments receive the penalty. This procedure should be followed even when it is inconvenient to administer it or in spite of the pleading of individual students that an exception be made. Obvious inconsistency in the use of procedures or in the application of penalties will cause confusion about what is acceptable behavior. Students will then frequently "test the limits" by not following the procedure or by repeating whatever behavior was to have evoked the penalty. These events can rapidly escalate and force the teacher either to abandon the procedure or to tolerate high levels of inappropriate behavior. Because neither outcome is desirable, it is best to avoid the problem by learning to be consistent from the start. Of course, it is not possible to be totally consistent; there will be occasions when the most reasonable course of action will be to make an exception to a rule or procedure. Thus, a deadline for an assignment may be extended when a student has a valid reason, or some procedures might be ignored during an emergency. Note that using certain procedures routinely for some activities but not for others is not inconsistent. For example, you may require that no students leave their seats without permission during discussions or presentations but you may allow them to get materials, sharpen pencils, or turn in papers as needed without permission during seatwork. As long as you have differentiated between the activities when you explain the procedures to the students, no problems should arise.

Undesirable inconsistency usually arises from three sources. First, the procedures or rules as presented are not reasonable, workable, or appropriate. Second, the teacher fails to monitor students closely and detects only a fraction of the inappropriate behavior. This creates the appearance of inconsistency. Finally, the teacher may not feel strongly enough about the procedure or rule to enforce it or to use the associated penalty. If you find yourself caught in an inconsistency that is becoming a problem, your alternatives are:

1. Reteach the procedure. Take a few minutes to discuss the problem with the class and to reiterate your desire that they follow the procedure. Then enforce it.

2. Modify the procedure or consequence and then reintroduce and use it.

3. Abandon the procedure or consequence, and possibly substitute another in its place.

Your choice of the alternatives depends on circumstances and the importance of the item to your classroom management system.

PROMPT MANAGEMENT OF INAPPROPRIATE BEHAVIOR

Inappropriate behavior must be handled promptly to keep it from continuing and spreading. Behaviors that you should be concerned about include lack of involvement in learning activities, prolonged inattention or work avoidance, and obvious violations of classroom rules and procedures. It is not a good idea to ignore such behavior: Prolonged inattention will make it difficult for the students to learn and to be able to complete assignments; violations of rules and failure to follow procedures create many problems we have already discussed. These behaviors should be dealt with directly but without overreaction. A calm, reasoned tone or approach will be more productive and less likely to lead to confrontation. The following alternatives are recommended.

Four Ways to Manage Inappropriate Behavior

1. When the student is off-task—that is, not working on an assignment—redirect his or her attention to the task: "Sammy, you should be writing now," or "Cynthia, the assignment is to complete all the problems on the page." Check the student's progress shortly thereafter to make sure he or she is continuing to work.

2. Make eye contact with or move closer to the student. Use a signal, such as a finger to the lips or a head shake, to prompt the appropriate behavior. Monitor until the student complies.

3. If the student is not following a procedure correctly, simply reminding the student of the correct procedure may be effective. You can either state the correct procedure or ask the student if he or she remembers it.

4. Ask or tell the student to stop the inappropriate behavior. Then monitor until it stops and the student begins constructive activity.

Sometimes it is inconvenient or would interrupt an activity to use these procedures immediately. If the behavior is not disruptive or is not likely to spread to other students, make a mental note of the problem and continue the activity until a more appropriate time occurs. Then tell the student you saw what was happening and discuss what the appropriate behavior should have been.

The four procedures outlined above are easy to use, cause little interruption of class activities, and enable students to correct their behavior. However, if a student persists in an unacceptable behavior, then some other alternatives should be used. If the rest of the class is working appropriately and does not need your immediate attention, then a brief talk with the student may be sufficient. If that doesn't settle the matter, or if an immediate conference is not desirable or feasible, stop the child's behavior and assess whatever penalty is appropriate. Some teachers use a "time-out" desk or chair as a holding area for erring students; others have students wait outside the classroom until time can be found for a conference. Before you do this, however, be sure school policy permits waiting in the hall. Note that the four procedures apply to relatively minor forms of misbehavior. Many additional measures to deal with problem behaviors are described in Chapters 7 and 8.

BUILDING A POSITIVE CLIMATE

This chapter has emphasized maintaining appropriate behavior by applying procedures and rules consistently, handling problems promptly, and using non-intrusive interventions when possible to maintain activity flow and student involvement in lessons. We now want to emphasize the importance of keeping a positive perspective and avoiding overdwelling on student misbehavior or inadequacies. Sometimes teachers get caught in the trap of seeing only faults and problems and overlooking the better features of students' behavior. Instead of rejoicing when 29 students are involved in learning, we complain about the one student who is off-task.

> Mr. Acerbic's sixth-grade physical education class could do no right. Although most of the students initially participated willingly in the class activities, students never seemed to perform quickly or well enough for their teacher. "Come on, you horseflies, quit buzzing and listen up," he would yell when he heard talking. "Laps" around the gym were given for even slight infractions such as inattention; there always seemed to be three or four students making the rounds at any given time. Instead of feedback about good performance, criticism was usually given for inadequacies. Although students took the constant carping in stride, they displayed little zest for the class.

Although poor performance should not be ignored—students need specific, corrective feedback in order to know what they need to improve—it is important that the climate for learning be positive. This means that students should look forward to the class. They should expect to learn and to receive assistance when they encounter difficulty and should feel supported in their efforts. Such a climate can be fostered by communicating positive expectations to students, by praising good performance, and, at times, by using additional rewards.

Teacher expectations can be communicated in a variety of ways, some obvious and others subtle. (For a thorough description of this aspect of teacher behavior, see Good and Brophy, 1987.) Teachers can:

- Identify appropriate instructional goals and discuss them with students so that they are clear about what is expected.

- Insist that students complete work satisfactorily.

- Refuse to accept excuses for poor work.

- Communicate acceptance of imperfect initial performance when students struggle to achieve new learning.

- Convey confidence in the student's ability to do well.

- Display an encouraging, "can do" attitude that generates student excitement and self-confidence.

- Avoid comparative evaluations, especially of lower ability students, that might cause them to conclude that they cannot accomplish the objectives.

By communicating positive expectations, teachers lay the foundation for students to attempt new tasks and reach new goals. When students know that their teacher believes them to be capable, they are more likely to try harder.

A positive climate for learning is also created by appropriate teacher praise. When used well, teacher praise can be uplifting and provide great encouragement to a student. The most powerful type of teacher praise provides the student with information about what aspect of student performance is praiseworthy and also demonstrates that the teacher is impressed with the quality of the student's work. In other words, effective praise provides both informative feedback and genuine teacher approval. It can also accompany suggestions for improvement (constructive criticism), without loss of effect.

For children from about the third grade and up, public praise that focuses on student accomplishment works better than praise for student effort. When teachers praise them for "working hard," many older elementary students are likely to assume that the teacher thinks they aren't very able. When you know that a student put forth considerable effort and you want to acknowledge it, be sure that the praise also includes an emphasis on the student's achievement. "Gloria, all your hard work paid off because your project was beautifully done. The organization of ideas and the extra details in the descriptions were outstanding!" Likewise, praise should be deserved and it should not be too easily obtained. Public praise of a student for success on an easy task can communicate to the rest of the class (and the student who was praised) that the teacher believes he or she has little ability.

It is a good idea to look for private ways to provide praise. Written comments on papers, tests, and other assignments offer excellent opportunities for quality praise. Private conversations, conferences with parents, notes home, and informal contacts also offer opportunities for praising students. Private praise avoids some of the complications of public praise, and permits the teacher to include a greater variety of performances and behaviors as the focus of praise. Further discussion of the uses of teacher praise can be found in Emmer (1988) and Brophy (1981).

IMPROVING CLASS CLIMATE THROUGH INCENTIVES OR REWARDS

Extra incentives or rewards can help build a positive climate. The improvement in class climate occurs because the incentives add interest or excitement to the class routine, while also directing attention toward appropriate behavior and away from inappropriate behavior. Moreover, students are more likely to respond positively to the teacher, contributing to a mutually supportive pattern of interaction.

Before using an added incentive, you should consider several factors that might affect its appropriateness and effects. You should check your school or district policies, because sometimes certain incentives are prohibited, and you would not want to promise a field trip or party only to find out that it was not allowed. Your rewards should target the behaviors you would like to encourage. Rewards too easily earned or too difficult to achieve lose their motivational effect. Also, you should be concerned about whether the use of a reward takes too much class time for record keeping or other administrative tasks. Avoid using complex systems that distract you and your students from a focus on learning. Start with simple procedures and add to them if that seems reasonable.

Be careful not to set up incentives that only the most able students can achieve. Systems that encourage excessive competition for scarce rewards will discourage those students who don't have much chance. The examples in this section and in the activities at the end of the chapter include a variety of types. Combine these ideas with those of other teachers and your own experience to develop some alternate rewards for use at various times of the year.

Many different types of rewards, including symbols, recognition, activities, and materials, can be used with elementary students. Each of these types is described below with examples.

Symbols

Elementary teachers use a variety of symbols to communicate a positive evaluation of student work. Examples include letter grades and numerical scores, happy faces, checks and check pluses, and stars and stickers with an appealing design. At all elementary-grade levels, the teacher's positive evaluation and written comments are a source of satisfaction for students. For younger children, especially, this reward should be provided as soon as possible after they complete a task and on a daily basis. Assignments in the early grades can usually be checked quickly, so there is no reason to delay feedback. One effective procedure for checking seatwork assignments such as worksheets, writing, or math is to

Reprinted by permission: Tribune Media Services.

have the children place them on a corner of their desks when finished. As you circulate through the room you can check completed assignments, write an E, put a star, check, or other symbol on the paper, and praise good effort, correctly done work, or neatness.

In the upper grades, where assignments are sometimes more complex or somewhat lengthy, you are more likely to collect assigned work in order to check it and record the grades in your grade book. Acquire a box of stars or other stickers, or buy hand stamps with a happy face or other symbols to supplement your numerical or letter grades. Be liberal in your use of these. Reward improvement and good effort so that all students have access to these incentives. Obviously, you should not reward poor performance, but do give feedback and encouragement so the student can improve.

In addition to their use for daily feedback, symbols are also used on report cards. Elementary-grade children, even first graders, place a very positive value on high grades (or "lots of E's"), and it is not uncommon to hear young children comparing report card grades. However, most first or second graders are not likely to have a very clear conception of a specific relationship between daily work and long-term grades. Consequently, report card grades are not particularly useful incentives for encouraging young children to complete daily work. In the upper elementary grades, however, students are better able to understand a connection between their work on daily assignments and the grades they receive in particular subjects. Therefore, it is a good idea to explain your grading policies to these children so that they will understand that the value you place on good effort and performance on daily work will translate into a report card grade. However, do not expect report card grades to be the major source of motivation for most students; plan to rely more on the daily use of symbols, positive feedback to students, and other rewards in the following discussions.

Recognition

Recognition rewards involve some means of giving attention to the students. Examples are displaying student work; awarding a certificate for achievement, for improvement, or for good behavior; and verbally citing student accomplishments. Recognition rewards may be given on a weekly or monthly basis using some system such as "Super Stars of the Week," a class honor roll, or "Good Worker's Award." Be sure to explain the basis for awards—for example, good attendance, achievement, improvement, hard work, good conduct, or citizenship. The more specific you can be when describing the desired behavior, the more likely you will be to obtain it.

Some teachers encourage competition among student work teams or other groups. These competitions may be very simple and short (for example, in a first-grade class the teacher might say, "Let's see which table is ready first!"); at higher grade levels competitions may run for a week, a month, or a grading term and may be based on behavior or some specific academic task. If competition among groups is encouraged, this fact should be kept in mind when the teacher forms the groups. Group composition should be balanced so that all groups have an equal chance to succeed. Competing for awards and prizes can be fun and will spur interest and effort. If you want to maximize the effect for all students, be liberal when giving awards—use second and third place and honorable mention awards so that everyone who participates appropriately receives some recognition.

Activities

Permitting or arranging for students to do something special or enjoyable constitutes giving an activity reward. Examples are privileges such as free-reading time, game time, visits to the school library, or appointment as a room monitor, game leader, or special helper. A more elaborate activity reward is the field trip or party. Because school policy may affect your use of the latter activities, you should clear any such activity with the appropriate administrator before announcing it to your class. You should, of course, be certain to describe clearly what students need to do to receive such privileges.

When activity rewards are used as incentives for the whole class, students can participate in their identification and selection. Thus, ideas for activity incentives can be solicited from students during a discussion, or the teacher might start with a short list and ask students to suggest additions to it; either way, the class can vote for a favorite. Some whole-class activities that might be used as incentives include watching a videotape, fifteen minutes of free time, playing a game, listening to music, having a popcorn party, or no homework. A group activity reward should be made contingent on specific desirable behaviors; if the group cooperates, then they receive the incentive. If not, then they lose some or all of the time in the activity. Because the purpose of using an activity reward is, at least in part, to promote positive climate building, it is important not to let one or two students spoil the fun for the rest of the class. A chronically uncooperative student can be invited to participate, but can be excluded from the reward if he or she persists in noncompliance. In most cases, however, positive peer pressure will encourage such a student to cooperate without the teacher having to resort to exclusion.

Material Incentives

Material incentives are objects of value to students. Examples include food, a pencil or eraser, discarded classroom materials, games, toys, or books. You will have to consider your own financial circumstances as well as school policy before deciding to use such rewards.

A procedure combining several types of rewards is the use of an honor roll system (an all-star list, super stars, gold record club) or competition among groups or teams in conjunction with other incentives. Badges, stickers with appealing designs, food treats, activity privileges, or a party can be used as rewards along with the recognition of being an award winner. It is best to spread the honors around and include a good portion of the class. Do not give awards only for outstanding achievement; have awards for improvement, excellent effort, good conduct, and so on.

When using a class party or field trip as an activity reward, you will need to be particularly careful. If only half the class can meet the criteria you establish for receiving this award, you will also have to figure out what to do with a large number of unhappy students during the party or field trip. For such a reward, it would be better to establish criteria that all students could meet (such as good citizenship). In this way you can encourage a class norm for good behavior that is attainable by everyone.

A major consideration in the use of rewards is their feasibility. Some rewards require a great deal of planning, record keeping, or other preparation. For example, a field trip, party, or major group activity needs careful planning. If some (presumably a very few) students will be denied the activity, then arrangements must be made for their supervision. In addition, transportation may need to be arranged, other adults may be needed for supervision, and some expense may be incurred. Other rewards require very little preparation or effort. Examples are giving positive verbal feedback, placing a symbol or some other positive comment on an assignment sheet, and awarding simple privileges such as leading the line to lunch, passing out materials, taking up papers, and being a room monitor.

Between the two extremes of much effort and very little effort are a large number of rewards that require a modest amount of the teacher's time or effort.

These include things such as awarding free time for reading, play, or games; sending home a positive note to parents; awarding prizes such as a pencil with the school name on it; allowing extra time in the library or for some other activity; and establishing an honor roll or "Super Star" list. Don't try too much too soon in the way of reward systems. Systems that require extensive record keeping or constant attention or complex arrangements will be a substantial drain on your time. Start with simple procedures and add to them if you can. The case studies at the end of the chapter illustrate a number of possibilities.

CAUTION IN THE USE OF REWARDS

Some researchers (e.g., Deci and Ryan, 1985; Lepper and Greene, 1978) have urged caution in the use of extrinsic rewards by pointing out that in some cases their use may erode students' intrinsic motivation to engage in the activity that is rewarded. Results from their studies and other research suggest that receiving a reward for engaging in an activity or performing an altruistic behavior reduces subsequent motivation if the extrinsic reward is later removed.

Explanations of this dampening effect on motivation usually focus on the implicit messages that are communicated when individuals are given rewards. For example, an implicit message might be, "This is an unpleasant or boring task, so a reward is needed to get anyone to do it." Consequently, the recipient tends to devalue the rewarded activity.

Before concluding that teachers should never use incentives, however, it should be noted that research in this area has several limitations. Much of it was conducted in laboratory settings where the task and its accompanying reward occur on only one occasion. Also the rewarded tasks in these studies have been highly interesting ones, such as games or puzzles. Thus, the research setting and the tasks were not very representative of real classrooms. Furthermore, some research has found that incentives can actually enhance interest rather than reduce it. Bandura (1986) argues that the conflicting findings mean that the effect of extrinsic rewards on intrinsic motivation is weak and many other factors operate to influence the effects of the use of incentives.

The most reasonable application of the research results for classroom use of rewards is to be thoughtful about their use. No purpose will be served by rewarding activities that are already highly interesting to students. In fact, the evidence suggests that to do so will reduce motivation. However, many classroom tasks are not highly interesting, especially those in which extensive repetition is needed to produce skilled performance and learning. When student motivation flags, external incentives may be necessary to maintain engagement. Actually, the use of incentives is more desirable than lowering expectations and accepting poor performance, or resorting to punishment or threats.

Calvin and Hobbes   by Bill Watterson

Finally, when rewards are used, the teacher can counteract the potentially negative effects on intrinsic motivation by pointing out to students the usefulness of the skill to be learned, by choosing materials and activities that have high potential for sustaining interest, and by modeling and demonstrating personal interest and enthusiasm for the task.

SUGGESTED ACTIVITIES

1. Read the Examples 6-1 through 6-4 and consider how you might adapt these examples of reward systems to your own classroom.

2. Find out about school policies that will affect your use of rewards. Also, note any schoolwide system that you will need to incorporate into your own classroom procedures.

3. Review Checklists 2 and 3 in Chapters 2 and 3 and identify the rewards you intend to use with your major conduct and accountability procedures. By planning ahead you will be better able to explain these incentives and to be consistent in their use.

4. In Problem 6-5, Ms. Wade is encountering some problems maintaining her management system. Use the information in this and previous chapters to diagnose her problems and to suggest what she can do to improve student behavior. Refer to the key in the Appendix for other suggestions.

■ *Example 6-1: Shoot for the Moon* Ms. Hardy used a reward system called "Shoot for the Moon" to give feedback to second-grade students for behavioral and academic performance. She decorated a large bulletin board with blue paper, a large round moon, a few clouds, and a title, "Shoot for the Moon." Each child's name was written on a small construction paper spaceship. The spaceships were lined up at the bottom of the bulletin board at the start. At the beginning of the year Ms. Hardy discussed with her class the kinds of behaviors that would result in the movement of each spaceship closer to the moon. Daily completion of assignments and good behavior in the classroom, at lunch, and on the playground would result in the spaceship moving two inches closer to the moon. For bad behavior (such as misbehavior in the lunchroom or during instruction, not working in class, or not turning in an assignment) a student's spaceship would be moved one inch away from the moon. When students reached the moon, they were rewarded by being able to keep their spaceships decorated with a star. The teacher then started another spaceship for them at the bottom of the board. Sometimes students were required to reach the moon by a certain deadline in order to get a special reward such as a privilege or a popcorn party. Ms. Hardy was consistent in rewarding appropriate behavior each day and in penalizing inappropriate behaviors, and she also occasionally rewarded individual students for being especially quiet or helpful or for improving their work or grades. This worked well with students who had particular behavior or academic problems.

■ *Example 6-2: Regular Feedback* Ms. Harmony's class functioned smoothly and productively without many obvious rewards and penalties. Although she only occasionally rewarded individuals or groups with public compliments, Ms. Harmony maintained a high level of student involvement through interesting, well-paced lessons and assignments with a high level of student success, and by promptly returning assignments and giving students feedback regarding their work. She dealt with inappropriate behavior by brief verbal correction of students or short private conferences with individuals inside the classroom. Often she would simply mention what the student should be doing if all the rest of his or her work was finished. Ms. Harmony made extensive use of telephone contacts with parents to inform them of their children's progress and particularly to identify when a student was not completing assignments satisfactorily. She did this frequently during the first few months of the school year, with long-lasting results.

■ *Example 6-3: A Token Exchange System* Mr. Young used a variety of strategies, some simple and some elaborate, for encouraging appropriate behavior in his third-grade class. Throughout the year he used a system in which the class as a whole earned blue chips for good behavior and red chips for poor behavior.

When a monthly goal for the number of blue chips was reached, the class was rewarded with a treat or special privilege. Goals and rewards escalated during the course of the year, beginning with a class party at the end of the first month and culminating in a field trip to a state fair. During each day blue chips were dropped into a container for various appropriate behaviors—two for good behavior during the time a visitor was in the room, ten for each satisfactory cleanup, one for each student who at the end of the day had completed his or her contract work, and so on. Red chips were dropped into the container for excessive noise, throwing trash on the floor, bad behavior on the way to lunch, or other transgressions. Shaking the can that contained the chips was often used to signal that there was too much talking or misbehaving and that failure to get quiet would result in another red chip. At the end of the day red chips were counted and an equal number of blue chips were deducted from the blue chip collection.

In addition to the chip system, Mr. Young complimented good workers aloud, sometimes let best-behaved or best-prepared students line up first, put names of cooperative students on the board under a "Super People" title, and awarded happy faces to students who did all of their work that day.

■ *Example 6-4: Another Token Reward System*   Every Friday, Mrs. Smith used a special incentive system with her fourth graders. She cut out small strips from colored paper and used these as tokens for good behavior during the day. Good behavior was described ahead of time to students the first few times Mrs. Smith used the incentive system. At the end of an activity, she would pass out a strip to each student who had been attentive or on-task; if the activity took awhile to complete, she would give out strips during the activity. This would be accompanied by feedback about what was being rewarded: "I really appreciate how attentive everyone is being during this lesson;" or "Boys and girls, you are working so well on the assignment, I just know we are going to have a very good day;" or "I really like how everyone worked hard and cooperated during the group assignment, thank you very much." During the last thirty to forty-five minutes of the day, the teacher let the students trade in their strips for different treats during a Friday afternoon party. During the party, Mrs. Smith would provide an activity, such as a game or a short videotape of a children's program or cartoon, or she would read a story. The children enjoyed and looked forward to this end-of-week activity, and it assisted Mrs. Smith in obtaining very good effort and participation during her regular Friday academic activities.

Mrs. Smith also used special award certificates for individual students (booklets of certificates that can be copied can be purchased in school supply stores). These certificates were especially impressive because each was signed by the principal as well as by Mrs. Smith. Students were recognized for outstanding effort, improvement, or accomplishment. The certificates were awarded both publicly and privately.

? PROBLEM 6-1

Misbehavior in a Third-Grade Class. Ms. Wade's third-grade students never seem to settle down for very long. Regardless of whether the children have been assigned seatwork or are supposed to be paying attention to a presentation, some degree of commotion or noise is always present. During the first few days of school the class seemed well behaved and was seldom out of order, and almost all the children were cooperative and did their work. Gradually, however, more and more inappropriate socializing, loud talk, call-outs, and other interruptions occurred, even from previously quiet students.

During Ms. Wade's presentations to the class, students are frequently inattentive, and she is able to complete lessons only with difficulty. Sometimes she even stops lessons short because the children are so difficult to control. At times the only way she can restore a semblance of quiet is to start writing names on the board and assigning detention. However, even that tactic doesn't work for very long because so many students are inattentive that the list of names gets very long and not being on the list becomes something of a social stigma.

During a recent reading-group period, three students talked continuously while Ms. Wade was working with one of the small groups. Two other children wandered around the room and a half-dozen others made frequent trips to the drinking fountain, restrooms, and hamster cages.

What has gone wrong in this class? How might Ms. Wade attempt to gain better cooperation from her students?

7

Communication Skills for Teaching

Throughout this book we have emphasized classroom management's preventive and instructional aspects. Not all problems can be prevented, however, and sometimes unobtrusive handling of inappropriate behavior during instruction is not sufficient. The approaches described in this chapter provide some additional means for dealing with problems that persist. The example below illustrates such a situation.

During the past several days Debra and Diane have been increasingly inattentive in Ms. Harris' fifth-grade class. Their off-task behavior has included whispering with other students and each other, teasing boys seated nearby, and displaying exaggerated boredom with class discussions. Ms. Harris first asked the girls to stop bothering the class, and when that had no effect, she moved the girls to different seats. However, Debra and Diane continued to disrupt by passing notes and calling out loudly to one another.

We will not second guess Ms. Harris by wondering whether she had communicated expectations clearly or had taken action promptly enough: Let us suppose that she had, in fact, practiced good preventive management skills, but the students misbehaved anyway. No strategy works all the time! What options are now available to Ms. Harris to deal with the situation? Some possible approaches include the following:

- Ignore the problem and hope it goes away.
- Refer the students to the principal.
- Call the students' parents and ask for their help.
- Apply a consequence, such as detention or some other punishment.

Each of the above approaches has advantages and limitations. For example, ignoring the problem requires little effort and might work if the students are mainly seeking teacher attention. The description does not, however, suggest that this is a likely reason for the behavior and ignoring may only allow it to intensify and spread to other students. Referral has the advantage of demanding little of the teacher's time, at least in the short run; it also temporarily removes the disruptive students, and it can have deterrent value. However, it may do nothing in the long run to deal with the problem the students are causing in the class, and although referral may sometimes be a reasonable approach to serious misbehavior, it can easily be overused.

A telephone call to parents sometimes works wonders and is usually worth a try. However, parents cannot always stop misbehavior. They do not, after all, accompany their child to your class, nor do they control the cues that are eliciting the misbehavior. Punishing the students by assigning detention or withholding some desirable activity or privilege is another possible reaction. Punishment, as will be discussed in Chapter 8, can stop misbehavior, at least temporarily, and it can deter other students. But punishment can have the disadvantages of creating hostility or resentment and of trapping the teacher and students in a cycle of misbehavior-reaction that leads to power struggles. By itself, punishment does little to teach the student self-control and responsibility.

Because each of these approaches has limitations, you need additional means of coping with problems. This does not mean that other approaches such as ignoring, referral, applying consequences, or involving parents will be supplanted. It does mean that communication strategies should be added to your repertoire to deal with problems that cannot be corrected with minor interventions and to help students learn to take responsibility for their own behavior.

In addition to being helpful in dealing with students whose behavior is creating a problem for the teacher or for other students, communication skills can be used to assist students who are themselves experiencing problems. Teachers frequently become aware of students' problems caused by factors both inside and outside the classroom. Sometimes teachers can help these students by being good listeners and by encouraging them to consider alternate ways to solve problems or to adapt to difficult situations.

We use the label *communication skills* for the set of strategies described in this chapter to emphasize that the approach focuses on communicating clearly and effectively with others to help bring about a change in their behavior, in their thinking, or in the situation that has caused the problem. But communication also means being open to information, so teachers also need to be good listeners and to try to understand the student's (or parents') concerns and feelings. In order to become an effective communicator, three related skills are needed:

1. **Constructive assertiveness:** This includes describing your concerns clearly, insisting that misbehavior be corrected, and resisting being coerced or manipulated.

2. **Empathic responding:** This refers to listening to the student's perspective and reacting in ways that maintain a positive relationship and encourage further discussion.

3. **Problem solving:** This component includes several steps for reaching mutually satisfactory resolutions to problems; it requires working with the student to develop a plan for change.

The three elements are derived from a variety of sources, including Gordon's *Teacher Effectiveness Training*, Gazda's *Human Relations Development: A Manual for Educators*, Glasser's *Reality Therapy*, Alberti's *Assertiveness*, Zuker's *Mastering Assertiveness Skills*, and other standard references. Several of these books are included in the bibliography. The treatment of communication skills in this chapter is intended to be an introduction; if you are interested in further reading, we suggest that you refer to one or more of the cited books.

Although this chapter's treatment of assertiveness, empathic responding, and problem solving focuses on their use with students, the skills are very helpful when dealing with parents—especially during parent conferences—and other adults. Thus, the skills described in this chapter have a variety of applications and will improve your effectiveness in handling many classroom and school-related situations.

CONSTRUCTIVE ASSERTIVENESS

Assertiveness is the ability to stand up for one's legitimate rights in ways that help ensure that others cannot ignore or circumvent them. The adjective *construc-*

tive means that the assertive teacher does not deride or attack the student. Assertiveness can be thought of as a general characteristic or attribute that we use in a wide variety of settings or as a set of skills that are more situation specific. Some individuals are assertive in a variety of settings (e.g., interacting with strangers, on the job, at parties, in school, etc.), while others lack assertiveness in many social situations.

However, even if you are not generally assertive, you can learn to use assertive behaviors while you are teaching. In fact, doing so may generalize to other situations as you become more confident of your skills. People who are very unassertive (e.g., feel extremely nervous whenever they are expected to lead a group; are unable to begin conversations or to make eye contact with others; accede to inappropriate demands readily; are unable to ask others to respect their rights) will find teaching uncomfortable and will have particular difficulty with discipline. Such people can help themselves in several ways, especially by reading about assertiveness and practicing some of the skills, preferably in situations that are not too uncomfortable, until they begin to develop more confidence. It is also possible to obtain professional help, such as from a counseling center, or to enroll in a course or workshop on assertiveness training. A good training program will usually include cognitive restructuring to reshape negative thought patterns that interfere with appropriate social interaction, anxiety-reduction exercise, and skills training and practice to develop more effective behaviors.

The elements of assertiveness include:

- A clear statement of the problem or issue

- Unambiguous body language

- Insistence on appropriate behavior and resolution of the problem

  Assertiveness is not:

- Hostile or aggressive

- Argumentative

- Inflexible

- Wimpy, wishy-washy, doormat behavior

Assertiveness lies on a continuum of social response between aggressive, overbearing pushiness and timid, ineffectual, or submissive responses that allow some students to trample on the teacher's and other students' rights. Assertiveness skills allow you to communicate to students that you are serious about teaching and about maintaining a classroom in which everyone's rights are respected.

We will now consider aspects of constructive assertiveness that have special importance for teachers.

Stating the Problem or Concern

Student misbehavior usually causes problems for teachers by making it difficult to conduct lessons, by slowing down activities, by subverting routines that help a class run smoothly, and by distracting other students from their work. When misbehavior persists, it is time for the teacher to let the student know what the problem is, from the teacher's point of view. Sometimes just a simple description of the problem may result in students' changing their behavior because they become more aware of it and begin to monitor it better. Stating the problem has two parts: (1) identifying the student behavior and (2) describing its effects as in the following examples:

"Talking and passing notes during discussion distracts other students from the lesson."

"Please raise your hand so that I can call on you."

"Wandering around the room disturbs the class."

"Calling other students names causes hard feelings."

By focusing on the behavior and its effects you can reduce the potential for student defensiveness and keep open the opportunity for achieving a satisfactory resolution to the situation. Conducting the conference privately (e.g., after class or during a conference period) when possible will lessen the potential for embarrassing the student in front of peers and will reduce the likelihood of a confrontation or power struggle that challenges the teacher's authority. Sometimes you will be forced to act immediately when a private conference is not an option. Choose these times well because public confrontations send messages to students about boundaries.

Notice that the problem descriptions above do not label students or their behavior; that is, students are not accused of being bad, rude, and annoying or behaving in an inconsiderate and stupid manner. Such labeling, whether for a student or the student's behavior, should be avoided because it impedes behavior change by suggesting that a student's behavior is a permanent characteristic that the student might accept as valid. Notice also that statements rather than questions are used. Quizzing students (e.g., "Why are you talking?" "Do you think that you should be calling someone that name?") invites defensive, sarcastic, or oppositional responses and can result in arguments.

Body Language

Constructive assertiveness with students needs the visual reinforcement of appropriate body language in three areas. The first is making eye contact when addressing the student, especially when describing the problem and when calling for behavior change. Note that there is a difference between eye contact that communicates seriousness and resolve and an angry glare that emits hostility. Breaking eye contact from time to time relieves tension. A second area of assertive body language is maintaining an alert posture and body orientation toward the student (but not so close as to threaten the student). Maintaining an erect posture and facing the student communicates your attention and involvement in the conversation. A third area is matching your facial expressions with the content and tone of your statements (e.g., not smiling when making serious statements).

Obtaining Appropriate Behavior

Assertiveness requires that the teacher not be diverted from insisting on appropriate behavior. Students may engage in diversionary tactics in several ways: by denying involvement, by arguing, and by blaming others (including the teacher). When dealing with such tactics, remember: There are many reasons, but no excuses, for misbehavior. While it is possible that others contributed to the problem, the student needs to accept responsibility for his or her own behavior. It is important to listen carefully to and understand the student's point of view, but in the end, if the student's behavior is interfering with your ability to teach, the behavior must change. Thus, if a student begins to argue or to deny responsibility for the behavior, you should avoid being sidetracked; the bottom line is that the student's behavior is not acceptable, whatever the reason for it.

When working with students who are evasive or who are not taking matters very seriously, a little dramatic emphasis may help move them to reconsider the situation. Consider Ms. Harris during a conference with Debra and Diane:

> "I've asked you to stay after class because I'm very concerned with your behavior. Please sit down." (Pauses, looks at the girls.) "I had to stop class three times today because of your loud talking." (Rises from behind desk, voice slightly louder.) "I cannot teach when noise interferes with our discussions." (Sits down, looks at the girls.) "This cannot go on any more." (Calm, but serious.) "Do you think we can work out a solution to this problem?"

Being an assertive teacher means that you let students know your concerns and wants in a manner that gets their attention and communicates your intent to carry through with consequences and to deal with the situation until it is resolved. It is not necessary that you lose your sense of humor or treat students impolitely. A little humor can reduce tension, and treating students with courtesy models the kind of behavior that you expect of them. Developing a level of assertiveness that is comfortable for you and understanding how your behavior is perceived by others are important; working through the activities at the end of the chapter will help.

EMPATHIC RESPONDING

Another important communication skill is the ability to respond empathically to students. This skill shows you are aware and accepting of the student's perspective, as well as willing to seek clarification of it when necessary. Empathic responding helps keep the lines of communication open between you and your students so that problems can be understood and resolved in mutually acceptable ways. Such skills are especially appropriate when a student seems excessively concerned, under stress, or otherwise upset. As a teacher you need to be able to respond in a manner that helps students deal constructively with those emotions or at least avoids further discomfort or distress. Empathic responding can also be used as a part of the problem-solving process when dealing with students who must change their behavior. In such situations, students may be resistant and express negative feelings; the teacher's empathic response can then help defuse these reactions and increase acceptance of a plan for change.

Empathic responding complements constructive assertiveness. Whereas assertiveness allows teachers to express their wants, empathic responding solicits and affirms the student's viewpoint. The use of empathic responding skills does not imply that misbehaving students are entitled to "do their thing" without regard for others; rather, the purpose is to understand and take into account the student's views in order to reach a satisfactory solution. If the teacher shows some openness toward the student's perspective, there is a better chance of the student's making a commitment to change. Conversely, a teacher who shows no interest in the student's feelings is more likely to encounter defiant behavior and an unwillingness to cooperate or to accept responsibility.

Compare the following two episodes.

Episode A

Student: I'm not staying. You can't make me.
Teacher: You'll have to stay after school. You haven't completed your work.

Student: No, I can't stay.
Teacher: That's life. If you don't serve your time now, it's doubled. That's the rule.
Student: (Angry) I'm leaving.
Teacher: You'd better not.
Student: I'm going! (Student leaves.)

In the above episode, the teacher's response does nothing to resolve the situation. It's likely that the student is aware of the consequences of skipping detention, so the argument only provokes a confrontation, which the student wins, at least temporarily, by leaving.

Another way to handle the situation is illustrated below.

Episode B

Student: I'm not staying. You can't make me.
Teacher: It's true, I can't. It's up to you.
Student: I can't stay.
Teacher: Staying after school is a problem for you?
Student: I have to be at home right away.
Teacher: So it would be a problem for you to get home late.
Student: Right, we're going somewhere after school today.
Teacher: That's a difficult situation. Would you like to talk about what you could do?
Student: Okay.

In Episode B, the teacher avoids arguing with the student and instead acknowledges the student's concern and invites further discussion. The student responds to the teacher's approach by stating his or her concern more explicitly. Notice that the teacher's role in this conference is that of listener or helper, rather than opponent. Notice, too, that the teacher does not offer to solve the student's problem by dropping the detention penalty. Instead the student is led to consider what options are available. Of course, there is no guarantee that the situation will be resolved to everyone's satisfaction. Yet the approach at least offers the possibility of resolution, and it avoids the confrontation that occurred in Episode A. Further, it maintains the student's responsibility for dealing with the situation rather than giving the student yet another excuse for avoiding responsibility.

Empathic responding has several advantages. It provides the teacher a means of dealing with strong student emotions without taking over responsibility for solving the student's problems. At the same time, the strategy helps defuse emotionally charged situations. Often, intense feelings are transient and will persist only when fed by an intense response. By not reciprocating with similar emotional intensity, the teacher avoids fueling the fire. Also, the calm, empathic teacher serves as a good model for constructive problem solving.

Empathic responding has two components: listening skills and processing skills.

Listening Skills

Listening skills acknowledge or accept the student's expression of feeling or ideas. At a minimal level, the listener merely indicates attention. Sometimes just an interested look will encourage the student to continue speaking. Other examples of nonverbal listening behaviors are nodding, making eye contact with the speaker, and other body language that communicates openness to discussion. Verbal encouragement is indicated by utterances such as "Um hm," "I see," "Go on," "That's interesting," and the like. At other times a little more encouragement may be needed. A child who expresses feelings of rejection or discouragement and who needs reassurance may respond to a friendly touch, a pat on the shoulder, or a hug. Beyond this level of response, the teacher can invite more discussion with statements such as, "Tell me more," "I'm interested in hearing your ideas about this," "Would you care to comment?" "What do you think?," and "You've listened to my opinion. I'd like to listen to yours."

Processing Skills

Processing skills allow you to confirm or clarify your perception of the student's message. Consider the following interchanges and identify the one that would be most likely to lead to further discussion:

> *Student:* I can't do this assignment.
> *Teacher (A):* You're having difficulty?
> *Teacher (B):* Come on, try harder—you'll get it done.

> *Student:* (Tearful) I hate Angela. She's not my friend any more.
> *Teacher (A):* It's upsetting to lose a friend.
> *Teacher (B):* Don't be silly. She's your best friend. Just tell her you're sorry.

In these interchanges, the A responses are more accepting of the student's feeling, whereas the B responses ignore the student's emotional tone and tend to block further communication. The B comments are judgmental and suggest a solution, without obtaining enough information about the situation and without giving the students the opportunity to deal with their own problems.

To process student comments, you can often just repeat back or summarize what the student says. If the student has given multiple messages or a confusing array of statements, select what seems to be most important and paraphrase it. This paraphrase can simply be stated back, or you can "reflect" or "bounce back" the paraphrase as a question. Whichever you do, the student usually will either acknowledge the correctness of your perception or else offer clarification or elaboration. Consider the following interchange from a short afterschool conference:

Student: I hate this place. School is stupid!
Teacher: Would you like to talk about it?
Student: I just don't like it here.
Teacher: There's something about school that bothers you.
Student: (*Crying*) Yes. Sean and Billy laugh at me.
Teacher: (*Puts arm around student*) You feel sad because they're making fun of you?
Student: Yes.
Teacher: Can you tell me about that?
Student: They call me stupid and dummy.
Teacher: It hurts a lot to be called those names. Are you worried that they really think that about you?
Student: No. I'm not dumb.
Teacher: You're not, and I'm glad you don't think so. I don't think so either. Would you like to talk about what to do when someone calls you a name or makes fun of you?

In this example, the teacher uses a variety of responses with an unhappy student and progresses to the point where the student can express, at least partially, some of the basis for the feelings. The teacher can then offer to help the student learn how to deal with the problem. Although it is not realistic to expect that major problems will usually be resolved via a single empathic interchange with a teacher, it is not unusual for the sharp edge of negative emotions to be blunted and for the conversation to end on a positive note. At the least, the student will know that an adult cares enough to listen, and the teacher will be in a better position to guide the student in the future.

The skills of empathic responding—both listening and processing—have been presented in the context of interactions with an individual student, but they are also helpful when problems arise in group settings. In particular, using these tactics helps prevent teachers from responding defensively when students react emotionally or express a problem during class. They also "buy time" for the teacher to consider alternatives for dealing with a problem. In addition, listening and processing skills are useful for leading group discussions.

Although empathic responding skills are very helpful in some situations, they are not intended as the primary means of dealing with students who are acting out, breaking class rules, or interfering with other students. Such misbehavior needs to be dealt with using approaches discussed in Chapters 6 and 8 and in the other sections of this chapter. However, listening and processing can be used to support these other measures.

Another limitation in the use of these skills is that of finding the right time and place to use them. It would be awkward, to say the least, to respond empathically to every expression of emotion or opinion during class activities. Such reactivity would cause slowdowns and would undermine your students' attention to lessons. How frequently and in which circumstances you choose to use these skills will depend on a variety of factors, including opportunities, your goals and values, and how competent you feel. At the least you should develop your skills so that you are able to respond empathically in situations where the use of the skills would be helpful. Doing so effectively requires practice and observation, and working through the activities at the end of the chapter will help.

PROBLEM SOLVING

Problem solving is a process that is used to deal with and to resolve conflicts. Conflicts arise between teachers and students because different roles give rise to different needs and because individuals have different goals and interests. In a crowded classroom, diverse paths can cross and individuals can find themselves at odds with one another. If conflict arises, teachers need a way to manage it constructively so that teaching and learning can continue in a supportive classroom climate. An effective means of accomplishing this is the problem-solving process, in which the teacher works with the student to develop a plan to reduce or eliminate the problem. Steps in the problem-solving process include (1) identifying the problem, (2) discussing alternative solutions, and (3) obtaining a commitment to try one of them. Depending on circumstances, problem solving may also include attempts to identify the causes of the problem and may specify the consequences of following or not following the plan. Because it generally requires more than a brief intervention, problem solving is usually conducted during a conference with the students it concerns. Often, the skills of constructive assertiveness and empathic responding are helpful in reaching a workable agreement for solving the problem.

Problem-solving conferences are usually reserved for chronic situations that have not yielded to simpler remedies. Some action needs to be taken to stop the behavior because allowing it to continue would interfere with your ability to teach, with other students' opportunities to learn, or with the student's long-term functioning in your class or school. Consider the following examples:

1. Brad likes to be the center of attention. Whenever you ask a question he calls out the answer without raising his hand and with no regard for the fact that you have already called on another student. Although you have reminded him of correct behavior and have tried to ignore his call-outs, the behavior continues to interfere with your class discussions.

2. Alice and Alicia never seem to clean up materials, supplies, or their work areas when they have finished a project or assignment. They resent your reminders and insistence that they observe class procedures, but unless you monitor them closely they avoid all responsibilities. Lately they have been arguing and complaining whenever they are asked to complete a task. Their foot dragging seemed trivial at first, but it has become a constant source of irritation.

3. Terrence has skipped his last three arithmetic assignments, even though you allowed ample time in class to work on them. He seems to have a lackadaisical attitude about academic work, and he uses his time in class for goofing off whenever he can get away with it. Twice last week he was kept in from recess to work on his missing assignments, but he did not finish them and he resented the loss of his midmorning break. During the previous grading period he had several unsatisfactory grades on his report card, and skipping assignments is sure to prevent his making satisfactory progress in learning arithmetic skills.

Each of the above examples illustrates a situation that has reached a stage at which a problem-solving conference might be useful. In each case, routine interventions have not changed the student's behavior; in each case, more of the same teacher response is likely to result in a continuing power struggle or in a deterioration in the student's ability to behave constructively.

What is evident in the three examples is that the students are not accepting responsibility for their behavior. It may be that what is needed is a stronger consequence (i.e., a penalty) that is clearly tied to the misbehavior. In fact, this strategy can be an alternative discussed with the student during a problem-solving conference. But until the student makes a commitment to change the offending behavior, the use of punishment will probably be perceived as coercive and controlling rather than as a natural consequence of the behavior and thus may do little or no good. It also appears that the basis of the problem in each of the three examples is not totally clear. Why won't Brad wait his turn? Why can't Alicia and Alice follow simple clean-up procedures? Is Terrence having difficulty understanding the content or is some external problem the source of his reluctance to do his work? Giving the students a chance to discuss their situations might provide insights that would lead to better solutions. It would also permit the teacher and students to become more aware of each other's perceptions and possibly prevent the development of additional problems.

Steps in a problem-solving conference are described below.

Step 1:   *Identifying the problem.*   You can begin the discussion by stating the purpose of the meeting and asking the student to express his or her viewpoint. Obtaining the student's views will give you useful information for later steps, and it will also enable you to gauge the student's degree of cooperation and understanding of the situation. An alternative opening is to describe the problem yourself and ask the student for a reaction; this alternative is especially needed when dealing with young children, with students having limited verbal skills, and with evasive and dissembling students. Unless the student's attitude is very cooperative, you will need to be assertive in expressing your concerns. As explained earlier, this can be done by describing, without labeling, the behavior of concern and the problem it is causing. You may also need to stress that the problem will not be allowed to continue and that something must be done to solve it.

Glasser (1975) recommends asking students to evaluate whether their behavior is helping or hurting them or has good or bad effects. The logic is that a student who understands and admits that a behavior has negative consequences will be more likely to participate in the search for and commitment to a solution. A student who denies responsibility or who sees no harmful effects seldom makes a meaningful commitment to change. It may be helpful to ask such a student what might happen if the behavior continues.

During this initial phase of the conference, students may react defensively or emotionally, and they may try to avoid responsibility by blaming others, arguing, citing extenuating circumstances, and so forth. When such behavior occurs, you must decide if the student's reactions are primarily for the purpose of evading responsibility or if they have some validity. If the latter is the case, then you can use listening and processing skills to respond. This communicates willingness to hear the student's point of view and may increase subsequent cooperation. By modeling such desirable behavior, you encourage its use by the student. A disadvantage of using empathic responding during this phase of problem solving is that the student's excuses, arguments, and extenuating circumstances may simply be a means of avoiding responsibility. Because you do not want to get sidetracked from the issue that brought the student to the conference in the first place, be sure to return the focus to the main problem once student concerns have been expressed. When the problem has been identified and agreed upon, the conference can move to the next step.

Step 2:   *Selecting a solution.* One way to begin this phase is to invite the student to suggest a solution to the problem. If the student is unable to do so, then you can offer one. Whenever possible, it is best to have two or more alternatives so that options can be compared and the most desirable one chosen. Frequently, the student's solution will be stated negatively, focusing on simply ending an undesirable behavior. While this is a step in the right direction, it is best to include a positive focus as well by including a plan for increasing desirable behavior. Thus, you should be ready to work with the student's ideas and also to suggest modifications.

If you are the one who suggests a solution, seek the student's reaction in order to check whether the plan is understood and accepted. Also, evaluate the plan's appropriateness: Is it realistic? Will it significantly reduce the problem? Does it call for changes in other students or in the classroom environment, and are such changes feasible? Can it be evaluated readily? Occasionally a student may try to avoid responsibility by proposing a solution that places the burden for change on the teacher or on other students, for example, to design more interesting lessons or to get other students to "leave me alone." Consider such changes to the extent they are appropriate and reasonable, but don't allow a student to shift responsibility to others—unless, of course, that is where responsibility for the problem lies. A reasonable response is, "Yes, such changes would help, but what will you contribute?" Once a mutually agreeable solution is reached, you are ready for the third step.

Step 3:   *Obtaining a commitment.* In this step the teacher asks the student to accept the solution and to try it for a specified period, usually with the understanding that it will be evaluated afterward. The student's commitment can be given orally or in written form, as in a "contract." Sometimes contracts are printed with an official-looking border, seal, and script, with space for student and teacher signatures and for listing contract terms and consequences if the plan is or is not followed.

Whether or not consequences are specified in case the plan is not followed will depend on the severity of the problem and whether it is a first conference or a follow-up for a broken contract. Some teachers like to give students a chance to correct their behavior without resorting to penalties, the rationale being that long-range cooperation is better when the teacher uses the least controlling or coercive approach. However, if the student is not making a reasonable effort to comply with the plan, or if the misbehavior is dangerous or too disruptive to be allowed to continue, then spelling out the consequences may be needed to get the student's attention and to communicate the seriousness of the situation: "You will need to choose between following our agreement or discussing your behavior with our principal, Mrs. Dreadnought, and your parents."

If the plan fails to solve the problem, then you'll either need to follow through with whatever consequence was stipulated, or else you'll need to work with the student to alter the plan to produce a more workable solution. A major consideration is how much time and energy you can or should devote to pursuing the plan, versus using a referral, a detention, or some other consequence available in your school. You might also consult with a counselor, an assistant principal, or another teacher before taking further action, in order to get another perspective on the problem.

When problem-solving conferences fail to make progress (e.g., the student does not make a sincere commitment to a plan or simply does not cooperate), the teacher should evaluate his or her assertiveness and empathic responding skills before concluding that the problem-solving approach does not work with that student. Poor assertiveness skills—hostile, critical, or attacking behaviors—and their opposites—timid, tentative responding—will interfere with the problem-solving process. An excessively assertive, hostile style reflects a reliance on the teacher's power and cuts off communication. An unassertive, timid style abdicates authority and is easily ignored; the teacher is not seen as credible and students simply will not believe that he or she will insist on correct behavior or will follow through with consequences. A constructively assertive teacher, however, captures the students' attention and communicates seriousness of intent in changing the situation. Empathic responding communicates a willingness to listen to the student's point of view and permits the teacher to clarify and react to a student's statements without closing off further discussion. Such skills are especially needed during problem-solving discussions, because they allow the teacher to deal constructively with defensive student behavior. They also help to clarify solutions as they are discussed and to improve the chances of obtaining a sincere commitment to change.

When you use these skills, be patient and give them a chance to work. Often teachers use a problem-solving approach after a situation has become chronic or for behavior that has been established over a long time. In such cases, you cannot expect miracles; change may occur only gradually and imperfectly. However, problem-solving conferences can be helpful in many cases and should be a component of your set of management and discipline skills.

Examples of problem-solving conferences are presented in Case Studies 7-1, 7-2, and 7-3. In addition, exercises on problem solving are presented in activities at the end of the chapter.

SUGGESTED ACTIVITIES

Activity 7-1: Developing Assertiveness Skills

The purpose of this activity is to provide some situations for practicing assertiveness skills. For each situation described below, prepare an assertive response. Use the following sequence of steps with each situation until you are comfortable with the approach. Then combine the steps so that you have the experience of responding to situations.

Step 1: Write out a statement that describes the problem clearly or that insists that your rights be respected. Compare and discuss your statements with other participants. Revise your statement if you wish.

Step 2: Use role playing to portray the situation, with you as teacher and someone else as the student. During the role play, try to use appropriate body language (including eye contact and facial expression) to support your intervention.

Step 3: Get feedback from observers regarding your use of assertiveness skills. Use the Assertiveness Scales to assess your own behavior, and check out your perceptions by comparing your self-ratings to those of observers. Be sure to discuss any discrepancies and any problems you experienced enacting an assertive role. Repeat Step 2 until you feel comfortable with your handling of the situation.

It is not necessary to continue the role play to a complete resolution of the situation. The purpose is only to provide experience in enacting assertive behaviors. The person playing the student role should respond as naturally as possible.

- *Situation A.* Bubba has been sliding by lately, doing the minimum and barely passing. At the end of class today he asks you if it would be all right to turn in his project a few days late. He knows that you have already given similar permission to two other students who had difficulty obtaining needed materials.

- *Situation B.* Martha and Maria are supposed to put the equipment away, but they have left much of it strewn about the gym. Now they are heading for the door in anticipation of the end-of-recess bell.

- *Situation C.* Victor has not been working on his assignment. You caught his eye but he looked away, and he has continued to talk to nearby students. As you move around the room checking other students' progress, he begins to make a paper airplane.

- *Situation D.* As you walk down the hallway, you hear two students trading insults: "Your mama . . .!" etc. The students are not angry yet, just fooling around, but several other students are gathering and you think they may encourage the two students to fight.

- *Situation E.* As you begin class, you observe Donalda eating a Twinkie, in violation of the rule prohibiting food in the room. When she sees that you notice her, Donalda stuffs the Twinkie into her mouth and gets another one out of the package.

- *Situation F.* During your current events discussion, Jack and Jill trade notes and laugh noisily. You sense that other students' attention is being captured by the duo's antics, and you begin to be annoyed by having to compete for class attention.

- *Situation G.* When you were absent yesterday, your fourth-grade class gave the substitute teacher a hard time; according to the note she left for you (with a copy sent to the principal!), many students refused to work at all, four or five students left for the bathroom and didn't return until lunchtime, and a paper and spitwad fight raged most of the afternoon. As the morning bell rings, you enter the room to greet your class.

Activity 7-2: Recognizing Listening Responses

Each of the following dialogues depicts a statement and a variety of teacher responses. In each case, decide which one is closest to a listening response; i.e., invites further discussion or best reflects the idea or feeling. Check your accuracy against the key in the Appendix.

1. *Student:* School stinks.
    a. Don't use that type of language.
    b. You seem upset about school.
    c. Come on, things aren't that bad.
    d. That attitude will get you nowhere.

2. *Student:* I can't understand fractions. Why do we have to learn this stuff?
    a. You'll need it to get into college.
    b. Just keep at it. It'll make sense after awhile.
    c. Something isn't making sense to you?
    d. Would you like to come in for extra help after school?

3. *Student:* I don't want to sit near those boys any more.

   a. Sorry, but seats have been assigned.
   b. If they're bothering you, I can move you.
   c. Can you handle this on your own?
   d. What is the situation?

4. *Parent:* My child is very upset and needs more help or she won't be able to pass. She says she doesn't understand anything.

   a. Please go on. I'd like to hear more about this.
   b. She needs to pay closer attention in class.
   c. She's very anxious but actually she'll do just fine. She only needs to review more before tests.
   d. Most students find my explanations to be quite clear. Perhaps she isn't listening.

5. *Teacher next door:* My class is going to drive me up a wall. They have been impossible lately!

   a. Have you ever considered being more assertive with them?
   b. I know, everyone in this wing can hear them.
   c. They are really a handful!
   d. You think they're bad, you should have my group.

Activity 7-3: Producing Empathic Responses

You will need to work with a colleague during this activity. Take turns role playing the student and the teacher. The person role playing the teacher should practice empathic responding skills, and the student should try to behave as naturally as possible. Note that it is assumed that the dialogue is occurring at a time and place that permits this type of interchange and that the teacher is interested in allowing the student to describe the problem. These assumptions will not always be true, of course—you could not deal with these issues in the middle of reading groups, for example, nor will you always have the time to deal in this way with every student problem. In this exercise, you should avoid giving solutions for the student's problem; instead, concentrate on using listening and processing skills to encourage the student to talk about the situation and think through the problem.

- *Situation A.* Monica is an average student with poor writing skills. With tears in her eyes, she approaches you after class with an assignment you have given an unsatisfactory grade. "I thought that I did okay on this."

- *Situation B.* David, a bright student, offers you some advice: "This class would be a lot more interesting if we didn't have to do all these worksheets. Couldn't we choose our own work sometime?"

- *Situation C.* While the rest of the class is at work on an assignment, Barry closes his book, throws away his assignment sheet, and slinks down in his seat disgustedly.

- *Situation D.* For the second time this week, SueAnn has not turned in an assignment. Last week she "forgot" to bring her homework twice. Later, you remind SueAnn that assignments are important. "I don't care," she responds.

- *Situation E.* Armand, a new student, has been having trouble making friends. Lately he has been getting into arguments with some of the more popular boys, and he has been teasing a few girls, apparently to gain some attention. However, he has not succeeded in breaking into the social scene. After class one day he says to you, "I wish I could go back to my old school."

Activity 7-4: Problem-Solving Exercises

Use role playing to practice the problem-solving steps (identify the problem and its consequences, identify and select a solution, obtain a commitment to try it out) with the situations described below. In those situations in which the student is mainly experiencing the problem, assume that the teacher's initial listening response is received positively by the student so that there is a basis for continuing the discussion and for the teacher to assist the student in thinking through a solution. In cases in which the student's behavior is affecting the teacher's ability to teach or interfering with other students' rights, then the student may initially be reluctant to participate in this type of discussion, and the teacher will need to use assertiveness skills to overcome this resistance. In addition to the situations listed below, you can also use some of the situations presented in Activities 7-1 and 7-3 for additional practice.

- *Situation A.* Bob and Ray are noisy and distracting when they clown around and vie for other students' attention. Reminders and penalties have only fleeting effects on their behavior. Therefore, you decide to have them come in for a conference.

- *Situation B.* David is good natured as long as no demands are placed upon him. However, when reminded that class time is for learning and for working on assignments, he becomes defiant and insists that it is his right to do whatever he wishes, as long as he "don't hurt no one."

■ *Situation C.* Lucy is a bright student but often turns in work late; frequently it is incomplete. She is able to pass your tests, however, and she could easily be a top student if she were prompt and better organized. Recently you sent her parents a progress report because of missing assignments, and Lucy and her mother have come in for a conference to discuss the situation. Her mother wonders whether you will allow Lucy to make up the missing work in order to avoid making failing grades.

Activity 7-5: Dialogue Analysis

Discuss the three vignettes at the end of the chapter. To what extent did the teachers use the problem-solving steps, as well as constructive assertiveness and empathic responding? Were they appropriately used? What other approaches might the teachers have tried for dealing with these problems? What are their advantages and disadvantages?

VIGNETTES

The three examples illustrate the use of a problem-solving conference for the three problem situations described earlier in this chapter.

Dialogue 7-1: Brad

Teacher: Brad, I asked you to stay to talk with me because of a problem we've been having during discussions. Often when I ask a question you call out the answer without waiting to be called upon. Do you agree that this is happening?

Brad: I guess so.

Teacher: Can you tell me why that is a problem?

Brad: I suppose that doesn't give others a chance.

Teacher: That's absolutely right. I have to be able to find out whether other boys and girls understand what we are discussing.

Brad: What if they don't know?

Teacher: You mean, if nobody raises a hand or tries to answer?

Brad: Yeah, then can I answer?

Teacher: Do you suppose that some people might need more time to think about what they are going to say?

Brad: I guess so. But it's boring to just sit and wait for someone to think if I already know it.

Teacher: It is hard to wait and be patient. But I must be able to teach the whole class and to conduct the discussions for everybody. Can you think of any way that we could handle this so that I can call on others when I want to and you can still have your fair turn?

Brad: I suppose I could raise my hand.

Teacher: That would be a big help. I would really appreciate that. I think you have some good ideas and should have plenty of chances to answer. Brad, how often would you like to speak during our discussions?

Brad: I don't know. (*Pauses.*) Three or four times, I guess.

Teacher: That would be fine. How about if I guarantee you four times during each discussion? You keep track of the times you answer, and I'll call on you when your hand is raised. If I don't call on you sometime, you know you'll get your chances later.

Brad: Okay.

Teacher: How about our trying this for the rest of the week, and then we'll talk again and see if it solves our problem?

Brad: Okay.

Dialogue 7-2: Alice and Alicia

Teacher: Girls, I asked you to stay for this conference because I've been having to take more and more of my time to get you to clean up and to keep work areas neat. I wonder what you both think about this problem.

Alice: I don't know.

Alicia: I don't think we're so bad about it.

Teacher: It has become very frustrating to me. Do you remember that I had to remind you and wait for the jobs to be done?

Girls: Yes.

Teacher: Whose job is it to pick up materials and put things away?

Girls: Ours.

Teacher: Do you think we can find a way for those jobs to get done? (*Girls nod affirmatively.*) Do you have any suggestions?

Alicia: I could just do it without being asked.

Teacher: Okay. That is a good idea. Do you have any other suggestions?

Alice: We could ask someone to help us.

Teacher: That is an interesting idea. Do you know someone who wants to clean up your things?

Alice: I don't know. Probably.

Teacher: Would you like to help someone else clean up or put things away?

Alicia: Sure, it'd be fun.

Teacher: How about you, Alice?

Alice: Okay.

Teacher: Well, then I have an idea. How about if I let you both be my room helpers this next week. As soon as you finish your own cleanup then you can help me with jobs that I need to have done. How would that be?

Girls: Yeah!

Teacher: Okay. Let's try this out. Tomorrow when you have cleaned up, let me know. Then I'll tell you what you can do to help me. How does that sound?

Girls: Sure! Okay.

Teacher: I'm glad we had a chance to plan this, because now I have two room helpers and we will have our problem solved.

Dialogue 7-3: Terrence

Teacher: I have noticed that you did not turn in the last three arithmetic assignments. What seems to be the matter?

Student: That work is too hard!

Teacher: You weren't able to do the work.

Student: No. I can't do it.

Teacher: When I was going around the room during seatwork, I noticed that you were able to do some of the problems, but then you stopped working.

Student: That's 'cause I couldn't do them any more!

Teacher: I see. That's pretty frustrating. Do you know, that happens to other people, too. (*Student shrugs.*) Even teachers. Did you know that even teachers sometimes don't know what to do next?

Student: No.

Teacher: Even me. (*Student smiles.*) Do you know what I do when I can't figure out how to do something?

Student: You ask somebody?

Teacher: Right! Does that give you any ideas about what to do when you don't know what to do?

Student: Ask somebody.

Teacher: Sure. If you get stuck, then ask. Do you know who you can ask?

Student: You.

Teacher: That's right. And you can also ask anyone at your table if I am busy and you need help right away.

Student: Okay.

Teacher: Did you finish your arithmetic problems today?

Student: No. I need some help.

Teacher: Why don't you get your paper from your desk and let's see what the problem is. . . .

ASSERTIVENESS ASSESSMENT SCALES

When using the following scales, note that a midrange rating represents an appropriate degree of assertiveness. When rating your own or another teacher's behavior as either nonassertive or hostile, circle the descriptive term that best reflects the basis for your judgment, or write a note on the scale if the descriptors don't adequately capture your perception.

	Nonassertive	Assertive	Hostile
	1 _____ 2 _____	3 _____	4 _____ 5
Eye contact	Teacher avoids looking at the student.	Teacher maintains eye contact with student.	Teacher glares at student; stares student down.
	1 _____ 2 _____	3 _____	4 _____ 5
Body language	Teacher turns away, gestures nervously, trembles.	Teacher faces student; alert posture but not threatening. Gestures support statements.	Teacher crowds student, points, shakes fist threateningly.
	1 _____ 2 _____	3 _____	4 _____ 5
Message	Obsequious, self-denigrating; excuses student behavior; pleads with student.	Clearly states the problem or insists that the behavior stop. Makes own feelings known, may use humor to relieve tension.	Name calling, labeling, blaming, threatening, sarcastic, preaching, lecturing.

	Nonassertive	Assertive	Hostile
	1 _____ 2 _____	3 _____	4 _____ 5
Voice features	Tremulous, whiny, hesitant, broken, or too soft.	Appropriate volume, natural sounding, varied for emphasis	Voice too loud; shouts, yells.
	1 _____ 2 _____	3 _____	4 _____ 5
Facial features	Smiles inappropriately; nervous twitches and tics.	Expression suits message.	Excessive affect; contorted, disgusted, enraged expression.

8 | Managing Problem Behaviors

In this chapter we will describe a series of strategies for dealing with problem behaviors that you may encounter in your classroom. Although previous chapters have described preventive measures as well as tactics that can be used to manage inappropriate behavior, we think that it will be helpful to consider the full range of approaches that can be used. We hope that you will not encounter problems, especially serious ones, in large numbers. But as you work with children you will undoubtedly face difficult situations that must be dealt with to preserve the climate for learning or to assist a child in developing behaviors more compatible with group life and learning. The aim of this chapter is to pull together and organize a wide array of possible strategies from which you can select. By having a broad array of approaches to draw upon, you will be better able to choose one that fits specific conditions. Having some alternatives in mind is very useful too, in case your first plan doesn't work.

We hope that this chapter's concern with behavior problems will not be taken as a grim comment on the teacher's role. In particular, the extensive list of strategies in this chapter should be considered within the context of the other chapters in this book. We have advocated generally a positive, supportive climate with heavy reliance on preventive measures. Within that framework, however, we must be ready to deal with problems when they arise. With a variety of strategies at hand, we can tailor our approach to fit the situation, keeping interruptions to the instructional program to a minimum, and at the same time promoting positive student adjustment and productive behavior.

This chapter's focus is on problem behaviors rather than problem students. Only a small percentage of children exhibit maladaptive behaviors with such consistency and to such a degree that they warrant being labeled emotionally disturbed or behaviorally disordered. Most children do, however, behave inappropriately on occasion; we think that it is much more constructive in the long run to deal with the student's behaviors and help students learn how to behave, rather than impute internal causes for the behavior and assume that the student is restricted in the capacity to make good choices.

On occasion, problem behaviors result from stressors (e.g., abuse, a death in the family, parental unemployment, serious illness, or divorce) the child is experiencing at home or elsewhere. If a child's behavior changes or if inappropriate behavior persists after reasonable attempts to deal with it have been made, then a discussion of the situation with a school counselor, social worker, parent, or guardian is in order. Sometimes the child's previous teacher might provide additional information. When you talk with the child about what is happening, use listening skills (see Chapter 7) to try to understand the situation. Be empathic, but help the child understand that acting out will not help the problem. By all means, follow up if you discover that a situation outside the classroom is affecting the child's behavior.

WHAT IS PROBLEM BEHAVIOR?

The concept of problem behavior is very broad. Rather than enumerate all the possible misbehaviors that might occur in classrooms, it is more manageable to think of some categories.

Nonproblem

Brief inattention, some talk during a transition between activities, small periods of woolgathering, and a short pause while working on an assignment are examples of common behaviors that are not really problems for anyone because they are of brief duration and don't interfere with instruction. Everyone is the better for their being ignored. To attempt to react to them would consume too much energy, interrupt lessons constantly, and detract from a positive classroom climate.

Minor Problem

This includes those behaviors that run counter to class procedures or rules but that do not, when occurring infrequently, disrupt class activities nor seriously interfere with student learning. Examples are students calling out or leaving seats without permission, reading or doing unrelated work during class time, passing notes, eating candy, scattering trash around, and excessive social talk during seatwork or group work activities. These behaviors are minor irritants as long as they are brief in duration and are limited to one or a few students. We would not give them much thought except for two reasons: Unattended, they might persist and spread; further, if the behaviors have an audience, then not to respond might cause a perception of inconsistency and potentially undermine an important aspect of the overall management system. Moreover, if students engage in such behavior for an extended period of time, their learning is likely to be adversely affected.

Major Problem, but Limited in Scope and Effects

This category includes behaviors that disrupt an activity or interfere with learning, but whose occurrence is limited to a single student, or perhaps to a few students, but not acting in concert. For example, a student may be chronically off-task. Another student may rarely complete assignments. Or a student may frequently fail to follow class rules for talk or movement around the room or may refuse to do any work. This category also includes a more serious, but isolated, violation of class or school rules; for example, an act of vandalism or hitting another child.

Escalating or Spreading Problem

In this category we include any minor problem that has become commonplace and thus constitutes a threat to order and to the learning environment. For example, many students roaming around the room at will and continually calling out irrelevant comments make content development activities suffer; social talking that continues unabated even when the teacher repeatedly asks for quiet is distracting to others; and talking back and refusal to cooperate with the teacher is frustrating and may lead quickly to a poor classroom climate. Frequent violations of class guidelines for behavior will cause the management and instructional system to break down and interfere with the momentum of class activities.

GOALS FOR MANAGING PROBLEM BEHAVIOR

Several types of goals need to be considered. We need to judge short-term and long-term effects of any management strategy we choose. In the short term, the desired results are that the inappropriate behaviors cease, and the students resume or begin appropriate behaviors. In the long run, it is important to prevent the problem from recurring. At the same time we must be watchful for potential negative side effects and take steps to minimize them. Effects on the individual student or students causing the problem as well as the effect on the whole class should also be considered.

> Joel is talking and showing off to a group of students during seatwork. The teacher could squelch Joel by using a sarcastic put-down or a strong desist, but chooses instead to redirect Joel's behavior and stand close by until he is working on the seatwork assignment. The put-down or strong desist might get quicker results in the short run, but it may lead to resentment or even conflict if Joel tries a rejoinder. Redirection and proximity control take a little more effort, but do not have negative side effects. In addition, they offer more support for appropriate behavior.

The ideal strategy is one that maintains or restores order in the class immediately; in addition, and ideal strategy would prevent a repetition of the problem and result in the student or students subsequently behaving appropriately in similar situations. In practice, classrooms are very busy places, and we rarely have sufficient time to mull over the various options and their effects whenever a problem arises, especially in the midst of a crisis. If only there were a "pause" button on classroom events! The need for prompt reaction should not, however, deter us from evaluating the results of our efforts and from seeking alternative approaches, especially when our initial efforts do not meet with success. It will, therefore, be useful to have a repertoire of strategies to apply to various problem situations.

MANAGEMENT STRATEGIES

In this section strategies are presented that are useful for dealing with a variety of classroom behavior problems. The first several strategies can be utilized during instruction without much difficulty, require little teacher time, and have the great virtue of being relatively unobtrusive. Thus, they have much to recommend them, because they do not give undue attention to the misbehavior, and they do not interfere with the flow of instructional activity. As we move down the list, we encounter strategies that are more direct attempts to stop the behaviors and to do so quickly; however, the strategies have more negative features: They demand more teacher time, they may have unintended consequences on students, or they interrupt class activities. A general principle that is helpful in selecting a strategy is to use an approach that will be effective in stopping the inappropriate behavior promptly and that has the least negative impact. An implication is that minor problems should usually be dealt with by the use of limited interventions. As problems become more serious, the limited interventions may be ineffective in quickly ending the disruptive behavior and thus a more time-consuming or intrusive intervention may be required.

It should be emphasized that most elementary schools have prescribed procedures to deal with certain types of major problems and sometimes even minor ones. For example, teacher responses to events such as fighting, obscene language, stealing, vandalism, and unexcused absence are likely to be directed by school (or district) policies. Therefore, the beginning teacher must learn what policies are in force and follow them. When no specific policy is established for particular problems or when teachers are given latitude in their response, then the alternatives below will be helpful in guiding teacher action.

It is a given that preventive measures are more desirable than reactive ones. Thus, the contents of earlier chapters have mainly been devoted to setting up the classroom environment to eliminate the need for frequent recourse to major interventions. Notwithstanding such efforts, responsive strategies still will be needed. However, when teachers find themselves frequently using major interventions to deal with minor problems, it is time to reevaluate their expectations and their overall management and instructional plan and make needed modifications. To this end, reviewing suggestions for management presented in prior chapters and perhaps using the checklists to provide focus could result in changes that would help reduce the problems. Teachers should also be sensitive to the possibility that the source of the problem lies in frustration with content that the student does not grasp or with tasks that the student lacks skills to perform. When the problem is one of a poor fit between student capabilities and academic demands, then the source must also be addressed by developing more appropriate class activities and assignments or by giving the student more assistance.

If you have a special education student whose behavior is causing a problem, then you may find it helpful to discuss the situation with a special education teacher and to ask for suggestions. In particular, ask the teacher if the student has a special discipline program as part of an individual education plan (IEP). Sometimes such a plan will specify particular ways to respond to the student or give some useful alternative strategies. Even if no specific discipline plan is included in the IEP, you may be able to obtain some helpful ideas for working with the student.

We have compiled classroom strategies that have a wide range of application, but the list is certainly not exhaustive. Readers interested in additional sources for ways of coping with specific problems may find the book by Stoner, Shinn, and Walker (1991) helpful. Also, suggestions for managing problems that have reached a crisis level are provided in Pitcher and Poland (1992). Many of the recommendations in the latter book are for school level administrators or school psychologists, but there is much of value to teachers as well.

Minor Interventions

Nonverbal Cues

Make eye contact with the student and give a signal such as a finger to the lips, a head shake (no-no!), or hand signal to issue a desist. Sometimes lightly touching a student on the arm or shoulder will help signal your presence and will have a calming effect.

Get the Activity Moving

Often student behavior deteriorates during transition times between activities or during "dead" time when no apparent focus for attention is present. Students leave their seats, talk, shuffle restlessly, and amuse themselves and each other while waiting for something to do. The remedy is obvious: Move through the transition more quickly and reduce or eliminate the dead time. This entails planning activities so that all materials are ready and adhering to a well-conceived lesson plan. Trying to catch and correct inappropriate student behaviors during such times is usually futile and misdirected. Just get the next activity underway and direct students to the desired behaviors.

Proximity

Move closer to students. Combine proximity with nonverbal cues to stop inappropriate behavior without interrupting the instruction. Be sure to continue monitoring the students at least until they have begun an appropriate activity.

Use Group Focus

Use group alerting, accountability, or a higher participation format (see discussion in Chapter 5) to draw students back into a lesson when attention has begun to wane or when students have been in a passive mode for too long and you observe off-task behavior spreading.

Redirect the Behavior

When students are off-task, remind them of appropriate behavior. "Everyone should be writing answers to the chapter questions," "Be sure that your group is discussing your project plan," "Everyone should be seated and quiet unless you have been given permission to leave your seat or talk." If only one or two students are engaged in inappropriate behavior, a private redirection will be less likely to interrupt the activity or to direct attention toward the incorrect behavior. A redirection strategy that works very well with younger children is the use of group and individual public praise for appropriate behavior. For example, if several students are talking and inattentive at the beginning of a new activity, the teacher should identify students who are behaving correctly: "I see many students who are sitting quietly ready to begin. . . . I really appreciate the boys and girls who are ready for our next activity. John is listening, Donica is being very quiet, Oh, good, Demetrius, Richard, and Corby are ready. . . ." In most cases, off-task students quickly come around.

Provide Needed Instruction

Especially during seatwork or group work activities, off-task behaviors may reflect poor comprehension of the task. Check student work or ask brief questions to assess understanding; give necessary assistance so that students can work independently. If many students can't proceed, stop the activity and provide whole-class instruction. Next time, be sure to check comprehension before starting the independent work activity.

Issue a Brief Desist

Tell the student(s) to stop the undesirable behavior. Make direct eye contact and be assertive (see Chapter 7). Keep your comments brief and then monitor the situation until the student complies. Combine this strategy with redirection in order to encourage desirable behavior.

Give the Student a Choice

Tell the student that he or she has a choice: either to behave appropriately or to continue the problem behavior and receive a consequence. For example, suppose a student has refused to clean up properly after completing a project: "You may choose to clean up now; if not, then you are choosing to stay in during recess until your area is clean." To a student who continues to distract nearby students: "You may choose to work quietly on your assignment at your seat, or you will need to sit in the time-out area to do your work." The purpose of stating the consequence as a choice is to emphasize the student's responsibility for his or her behavior. Also, making the consequence clear increases the chance of the student choosing to self-regulate.

Use an "I-Message"

An I-message is a statement that describes the problem and its effects on the teacher, the student, or the class; it may also include a description of the feelings produced by the problem. The formula for an I-message is:

- When you (state the problem)
- Then (describe the effect)
- And it makes me feel (state the emotion).

For example, to a student who constantly calls out comments, the teacher might say, "When you talk without permission, it interrupts the lesson, and I get frustrated and resentful." It isn't necessary, of course, to follow the formula exactly; the main idea is to communicate clearly what the problem is and why it's a problem (e.g., "It's very distracting to me and to others when you wander around the room during seatwork.") The I-message can be combined with a brief desist or with redirection. A rationale for using an I-message is that students often act without much awareness of the effects their behavior has on others, and they will change if they realize that they are causing someone a problem. Also, by communicating directly with the student about the effects of the behavior, the teacher implies that the student is capable of controlling the behavior, if only he or she understands its effects.

Moderate Interventions

Strategies in the next set utilize mild punishment (or negative consequences) and act directly to stop the problem behavior. These strategies are more confrontational than the limited interventions described above and thus have greater potential for eliciting resistance. In cases in which the student's behavior has not become especially disruptive, it is desirable to use a minor intervention or to issue a warning to the student before using these interventions. Doing so will permit the student to exercise self-control and may save teacher time and effort.

Withhold a Privilege or Desired Activity

Students who abuse a privilege (e.g., being allowed to work together on a project, sitting near friends, or freedom to move around the classroom without permission) can lose the privilege and be required to earn it back with appropriate behavior. Sometimes teachers allow quiet talking during seatwork activities, and its removal can be an effective way to limit unproductive social behavior. Other teachers allow a class to choose a favorite activity or a short period of free time on one or more days each week as incentives. Time lost from such activities can then be a strong deterrent to inappropriate behavior at other times. Although withholding a privilege is a form of punishment, it usually has fewer side effects than punishment that requires directly applying an aversive consequence.

Isolate or Remove Students

Students who disrupt an activity can be removed to some other area of the room, away from other students. It is helpful to have a carrel with sides or at least a desk at the back of the room facing away from other students to discourage eye contact from the time-out area. If no suitable place is available, then the student may need to have time out in the hall outside the door, although not if your school has a policy prohibiting this because of the problem of adequately supervising the student.

Time out is a variation on the preceding consequence, in that it takes away the student's privilege of participating in the activity. It is a good idea to allow excluded students to return to the activity in a short time, as long as their behavior in time out is acceptable. Some teachers prefer to let the student retain some control over the return, using a direction such as, "You may come back to the activity in five minutes if you decide that you can follow our class rules." Other teachers prohibit the student from returning until the activity is completed or until they have a brief conference with the student.

A problem with time out is that some students may find it rewarding. They receive attention when it is administered, and it allows them to avoid an activity they dislike. When this occurs, you should switch to another strategy. Another problem is that a student may refuse to go to the time-out area. Usually this is a temporary problem; if you are firm, ignoring the student's protests and continuing with the activity, the student will go eventually. One way to move a recalcitrant body is to offer a choice: "You can either take time out or you take a walk to the principal's office. It's your decision."

Time out has another risk. Its use clearly identifies a student as someone who is excludable, and it may result in implicit labeling by the teacher, by other students, or by the excluded student. If used frequently with an individual student, it may cause resentment and anger. Therefore, be sure to provide opportunities for the student to resume full participation in the class, and use other strategies to promote appropriate behavior at the same time.

Use a Fine or Penalty

Sometimes a small amount of repetitious work is required as payment for inappropriate behavior. For example, in physical education, students may be required to run an extra lap or do some push-ups. In math, students may have to work some extra problems. The advantage of this type of consequence is that it can usually be administered quickly with a minimum of teacher time and effort. A disadvantage is that the task is being defined as punishing, and therefore the student's attitude toward the content may be negatively affected. Another problem with the use of fines or penalties is that their ease of use can lead to overuse, detracting from the overall climate.

Assign Detention

Another penalty that is commonly used is to require that the student serve a detention, either at lunch, during recess, or sometimes before or after school. Because of the logical relation between the problem and the consequence, this penalty is often used for misbehaviors that involve time (e.g., extended goofing off and time-wasting; behavior that interferes with instruction or student work time). Other common uses of the penalty are for repeated rule violations and for frequent failure to complete assignments. You may need to supervise the detention in your room, or your school might have a detention hall with an assigned monitor. The time in detention need not be lengthy, especially for misbehaviors that are not severe or frequent; a ten or fifteen minute detention is often sufficient to make the point.

An advantage of detention as a penalty is that it is disliked by most students and they want to avoid it; at the same time, it is administered away from other students in the class and thus does not give undue attention to the behavior. Also, it is a common punishment, so extensive explanations and unusual procedures aren't needed. Finally, the teacher can sometimes use a little of the detention time to hold a conference with the student and perhaps work out a plan for improving the situation.

A disadvantage of detention is that it does take teacher time, especially when the teacher must supervise it. Even when the school has a D-Hall, the teacher still will need to write a referral. Another disadvantage is that students might be able to avoid detention, at least in the short run, simply by not showing up. Thus, the teacher or the school must have a backup plan, such as doubling the time; moreover, records must be kept and often additional time will be required to deal with such students.

Use a School-Based Consequence

If your school has a prescribed consequence for particular problem behaviors and you are allowed some latitude in its administration, you should consider utilizing it after you have not had desired results with other strategies. For example, some schools have a system of referral to the principal, who then deals with the student. Often, a first referral consequence is limited to detention or to a warning, with subsequent referrals resulting in a parent conference. It is necessary to apprise the administrator of the basis for the referral and to discuss what outcome is desirable. An advantage of this approach is that it does not require much teacher time. A disadvantage is that the usefulness of this strategy is dependent on others for its effectiveness; also, extensive and frequent external support for handling in-class problems is not a realistic option in most schools.

More Extensive Interventions

When students do not respond to minor or moderate interventions and their behavior continues to disrupt classroom activities and to interfere with their own and others' learning, one or more of the strategies described below can be helpful in reducing the inappropriate behaviors and allowing the teacher to re-establish a focus on learning.

Individual Contract with the Student

When a student's inappropriate behavior has become chronic or if a problem is severe and must stop immediately, try an individual contract. You will need to discuss the nature of the problem with the student, including the student's perspective on it. Then you and the student can identify appropriate solutions and agree on which course of action to take. Typically, the contract specifies changes the student will make, but it might also call for the teacher to alter some behavior or activity. You should also make clear what consequences will occur if the plan is not followed, and you can also identify some incentive to encourage the student to follow through with the contract. The plan and consequences are written down and signed by the student. Contracts can also be used with other strategies (see the Five-Step Plan and the Reality Therapy sections below).

Conference with a Parent

Sometimes a telephone call to a parent can have a marked effect on a student's behavior, signaling to the child that accountability for behavior extends beyond the classroom. Parents react best if they don't feel that they are being held responsible for their child's behavior in school (after all, they aren't there), so don't put the parent on the defensive. Describe the situation briefly and say that you would appreciate whatever support the parent can give in helping you understand and resolve the problem. Acknowledge the difficulty in rearing children as well as teaching them. Be sure to use listening skills (see Chapter 7) during the conversation and be alert for information that might help you determine an appropriate strategy for dealing with the student. Have your grade book handy so that you can give the parent specific information about the student's progress, if the information is requested or needed.

Rather than a phone conference, you might need to schedule a face-to-face conference with a parent. Sometimes, but by no means always, when such conferences are arranged it is because a problem has become quite severe, and other school personnel (e.g., a counselor or principal) may need to be present. If you have initiated the meeting, you should try to brief the others and plan your approach ahead of time.

The chief drawback to parent conferences is the time and energy they require. The effort is frequently worth it; although not every conference is successful, many times the student's behavior will improve. Another potential problem is identifying ahead of time what strategy would be best to follow with the parent. Occasionally parents overreact and punish children excessively. As the year progresses, you will get to know parents better and be able to gauge the probable effects of your call or conference.

Use a Check or Demerit System

This approach is used with the entire class; it requires the teacher to give a check or demerit when a student violates some rule or rules. If a student persists in the misbehavior, then additional checks are given. A specific penalty is attached to receiving one or more checks, for example, fifteen minutes of detention. An example of this approach is the "name-on-the-board" system. The teacher provides a list of rules to the students and informs them of the consequences of violations. A typical plan would be for the teacher to write the student's name on the board after the first violation, put a check mark after the second infraction, and so on. Associated consequences would be a warning for the name-on-the-board, followed by fifteen minutes' detention after each check. More severe penalties are added after the third check (e.g., call the parents or send the student to the principal). The student starts with a clean slate each day. More recently, Canter (1980) has suggested using a clipboard instead of the chalkboard to record student names. This latter approach is a better one to use, especially considering the possibility of a child being labeled as "bad" by peers when his or her name appears frequently on the board. Children's self-concepts are susceptible to such labeling effects, and teachers must be careful not to inadvertently encourage the development of a negative self-identity.

A variation on this procedure is a demerit system in which rule violations are recorded on a form which the teacher retains in a file folder for each class. In this approach, a record is maintained by the teacher and the student is required to sign the form acknowledging responsibility. Consequences initially are mild, but after several infractions in a given period of time, detention, a parent conference, or a behavior contract might be used. Students can be allowed to erase demerits with good behavior; e.g., no rule violations during a day.

An advantage of these systems is that they can help teachers set and maintain limits consistently. In addition, they make the consequences of rule violations clear to students and thus increase the predictability of the classroom environment. There are, however, several potential disadvantages. Probably the chief problem is the emphasis on catching students being bad. Whether the student's name goes on the chalkboard, clipboard, or on a piece of paper, attention is directed at the misbehavior. This may not be a major drawback if checks or demerits aren't given frequently and if the teacher is careful also to give students positive attention. If, however, many checks or demerits are given, then not only are misbehaviors receiving attention, but the flow of the lesson will be impeded, compounding the problem. Finally, if the inappropriate behaviors are not easy to observe accurately, then it will be very difficult to appear consistent in the use of the system. For example, trying to manage side talk during seatwork with this approach would be impossible in many classrooms, because it is too hard to detect each time it occurs.

Teachers sometimes adopt the name-on-the-board strategy as a last resort when student misbehaviors have become frequent and they believe they are in danger of losing control of a class. Unfortunately, it is under these conditions that this type of consequence system is most likely to break down, because the teacher spends excessive time attending to inappropriate behavior and to punishing students. If a class has become unruly, we suggest choosing one activity (e.g., seatwork or content development) and targeting for this system only one or two easily observable but problematic behaviors (e.g., being out of seat without permission, continuing to talk after being asked to stop). Students should know exactly what behaviors are not allowed and also what behaviors are desired. The system should be used only in that specific activity (i.e., not for the entire day) to avoid the teacher's having to play the role of "sheriff" all the time. The activity should be kept short and briskly paced during the first several days of implementation to increase the chances of success. Attention should also be provided for appropriate behaviors and appreciation should be communicated for students' greater maturity and improved behavior. When student behavior is under reasonable control in the selected activity, the system can be used in another activity if necessary.

Use Problem Solving

Because problem solving was described extensively in Chapter 7, it will not be discussed in this chapter. However, the next two strategies, which share some features with problem solving, are sufficiently unique to warrant a separate presentation.

Use a Five-Step Intervention Procedure

Jones and Jones (1990) recommend following five steps when dealing with disruptive student behavior.

Step 1: Use a nonverbal signal to cue the student to stop.
Step 2: If the behavior does not cease, then ask the student to follow the desired rule.
Step 3: If the disruption continues, give the student a choice of stopping the behavior or choosing to develop a plan.
Step 4: If the student still does not stop, then require that the student move to a designated area in the room to write a plan.
Step 5: If the student refuses to comply with Step 4, then send the student to another location (e.g., the school office) to complete the plan.

The use of the five-step intervention process requires a form for the plan (Figure 8-1). When the approach is introduced to the students, preferably at the beginning of the year, the teacher explains its purpose and how to fill out the form. Role playing the use of the five steps is recommended, both to teach the procedures and to provide a positive model of their application. It will also be helpful to laminate a couple of examples of appropriate plans so that students have models.

Advantages of this approach include its emphasis on student responsibility and choice. Also, a graduated response to the problem allows the teacher to intervene nonpunitively at first, and thus provides a means of settling the matter quickly with a minimum of disturbance to the on-going activity. The steps are simple and straightforward, which will promote consistency in their use by the teacher; students, in turn, will be aided by the structure and predictability of the approach.

A disadvantage of the system is that movement from Step 1 to Step 5 can occur very rapidly and some intermediate strategies may be necessary to avoid excessive reliance on sending students out. In addition, some students, especially in early primary grades, will have difficulty writing an acceptable plan by themselves. Finally, setting up the system and, later, meeting with students to discuss their plans and monitoring implementation require at least a moderate investment of time.

Use the Reality Therapy Model

William Glasser's (1975, 1977) ideas have been widely applied in education. Some of his recommendations for dealing with disruptive or maladaptive behaviors in a classroom setting are presented on the next page.

The essential features of using a Reality Therapy strategy when working with an individual student include establishing a caring relationship with the students,

---

CHOOSE TO BE RESPONSIBLE

Name _____ Date _____

Rules we agreed upon

1. Speak politely to others.
2. Treat each other kindly.
3. Follow teacher requests.
4. Be prepared for class.
5. Make a good effort at your work and request help if you need it.
6. Obey all school rules.

Please answer the following questions:

1. What rule did you violate? _____
   _____

2. What did you do that violated this rule? _____
   _____

3. What problem did this cause for you, your teacher, or classmates? _____
   _____

4. What plan can you develop that will help you be more responsible and follow this classroom rule? _____
   _____

5. How can the teacher or other students help you?
   _____

I, _____ , will try my best to follow the plan I have written and to follow all the other rules and procedures in our classroom that we created to make the classroom a good place to learn.

FIGURE 8-1. Problem-Solving Form
From Vernon F. Jones and Louise S. Jones, COMPREHENSIVE CLASSROOM MANAGEMENT: MOTIVATING AND MANAGING STUDENTS, Third Edition. Copyright © 1990 by Allyn and Bacon. Reprinted with permission.

focusing on the present behaviors, getting the student to accept responsibility, developing a plan for change, obtaining a commitment to follow the plan, and following up. Glasser believes strongly that students choose behavior depending on their perceptions of its consequences. Most students will choose appropriate behaviors when they believe these will lead to desirable outcomes and they will avoid behaviors that they perceive will lead to undesirable consequences. Glasser's plan can be put into effect by following the following steps.

Step 1: Establish involvement with the students. If students believe that the teacher cares for them and has their best interests in mind, then they will be more likely to follow the teacher's guidance when evaluating and changing their behavior. Teachers can show commitment to and caring for students in numerous ways: commenting favorably to the students about their work; being friendly; and showing an interest in different students' activities, family, likes and dislikes, and hobbies. Teachers can also get involved by demonstrating school spirit, joking, being a good listener, and taking time to talk with students about their concerns. The best time to establish involvement is before a student becomes disruptive, but even if a student has begun to exhibit problem behavior, it is not too late to begin. When a teacher makes a special effort just to have two or three friendly contacts a day with such a student, it can be helpful in creating a more positive climate for change.

Step 2: Focus on behavior. When a problem has occurred, Glasser recommends that a brief conference be held with the student. The initial concern should be to determine what the problem is. To this end, the teacher should ask only questions about "what happened" or "what's going on" and avoid trying to fix blame. Even if the teacher knows exactly what the problem is, it is wise to obtain the student's perspective.

Step 3: The student needs to accept responsibility for the behavior. This means that the student acknowledges that he or she did engage in the behavior. No excuses are accepted. Admitting responsibility is difficult, especially when there are so many other handy things to blame, but in the end, it is a form of denial to try to assign responsibility elsewhere when it was the student who engaged in the behavior. Of course, it is possible that more than one individual is responsible for the problem, but that should not be an excuse for irresponsibility.

Step 4: The student should evaluate the behavior. If students have difficulty perceiving their part or they minimize it, Glasser suggests asking, "Has the behavior helped or hurt you? Has it helped or hurt others?" The teacher may need to point out the negative consequences of continuing to misbehave. Unless the student sees that the behavior will lead to negative consequences and that changing it will produce desirable consequences, there isn't much reason to expect a change.

Step 5: Develop a plan. The teacher and student need to identify ways to prevent the problem from recurring, and what new behaviors are needed. The plan can be written as a contract.

Step 6:   The student must make a commitment to follow the plan. Progress will be limited at best if students do not seriously intend to make a change. It may help if the teacher makes clear the positive and negative consequences of following or not following the plan. The plan needs to be do-able in a reasonable time.

Step 7:   Follow-up and follow through. If the plan doesn't work, it should be modified with the student; if a negative consequence was called for in the plan it should be used. Glasser also proposes several additional steps beyond the classroom if a student continues to be a problem. For example, use of in-school suspension could be a consequence of continuing misbehavior; before the student is allowed to return to the classroom, an acceptable plan would need to be agreed upon. Only after several attempts to obtain a change have failed should the teacher refer the student to the principal.

The Reality Therapy approach to dealing with individual discipline problems has much to recommend it. It is a systematic way for teachers to deal with many kinds of individual student problems, and it provides a simple, yet effective, process for getting right at the issues, and avoiding being sidetracked by fault finding, conning, or excuse making. Research on the effects of this aspect of Reality Therapy is generally supportive (Emmer and Aussiker, 1990) for applications to individual students.

SPECIAL PROBLEMS

Children sometimes behave in ways that require stronger measures than those described in the preceding sections. Some of these behaviors include rudeness toward the teacher, chronic avoidance of work, fighting, other aggressive behavior, and defiance or hostility toward the teacher. While these behaviors are not pleasant to contemplate, they are an inevitable result of close contact with up to thirty children for long periods of time. Fortunately, few teachers encounter these behaviors in large amounts. Regardless of their frequency, you should be aware of ways to cope with them if they should occur.

Before discussing each type of problem, some general guidelines applicable to aggressive behaviors will be considered. You should think of coping with these behaviors in two phases: the immediate response and a long-range strategy. At the time you encounter the behavior, your immediate concern will be to bring it to a halt with a minimum of further disruption. Because these behaviors are annoying and frequently arouse anxiety or anger, you will need to be careful not to exacerbate the problem. Stay calm and avoid overreaction. Thinking about ways to handle disruptive behavior ahead of time will help you to act and not react. You can tell the student how you feel, but avoid an argument or an emotional confrontation. Then you will be in a better position to deal with the student and his or her problem. Long-range considerations are to prevent a recurrence of the behavior and to help the student learn a more constructive means of dealing with others. Preventing a recurrence of the behavior is best accomplished (1) by finding out what triggered the incident and dealing with the cause if possible, and (2) by having a predictable classroom environment, with reasonable and consistently used rules, procedures, and consequences. Such classrooms rarely have large amounts of aggressive behaviors. Helping a child acquire better behavior may require dealing with the student on an individual basis over a period of time. The extent to which this goal is feasible is, of course, limited by many factors, including your time constraints and the severity of the child's problem. In dealing with chronic problems, the child's parents and professionals such as the school counselor, a special education resource teacher, or the principal may be able to assist you. In the discussion below some suggestions for handling different types of behavior are presented.

Tattling

While tattling is often not a disruptive behavior, it can nevertheless become a problem in some classrooms when students make it a common practice. Most teachers in the early grades develop standard policies for dealing with tattling and apply these when it happens. In deciding how you will handle it, you should keep in mind that tattling is usually a bid for attention, and students who do this are usually seeking attention from the teacher. If tattlers are successful in getting you to intervene with the alleged misbehavior, it is likely that other students will follow suit. It is usually sufficient to remind the tattler of what he or she is supposed to be doing at that moment and have him or her return to it. It is also probably prudent for you to follow up and check out the situation for yourself.

Rudeness Toward the Teacher

Rudeness may take the form of sassy back talk, arguing, crude remarks, or gesturing. An important consideration in this type of behavior is not to overreact or argue with the student. Frequently, the child is using such behavior as a means of getting attention either from you or from peers, so you should avoid getting yourself trapped in a power struggle. To some extent your response will depend on the degree of rudeness and how public it was. In borderline cases the student may not even realize that a comment was offensive. A reasonable first reaction is to inform the student that the behavior is not acceptable and to refer to a general classroom rule such as "respect others" or "be polite." If the incident is repeated or if the original comment was intentionally rude, then some type of penalty should be used and/or the teacher should have a conference with the student. In the case of obnoxious behavior that disrupts the class or that persists, the student should be isolated from the other students or sent to the school office and not allowed to return until he or she agrees to behave appropriately. Most schools have a standard policy for dealing with extreme cases, and you should use whatever procedures have been established.

Chronic Avoidance of Work

You may have students who frequently do not complete assigned work. Sometimes they fail to complete assignments early in the school year; more often a student will begin to skip assignments occasionally and then with increasing regularity until he or she is habitually failing to do them. This behavior can be minimized by a carefully planned accountability system (review Chapter 3 for details). However, even in classrooms with a strong accountability system, some students may still avoid work.

It is much easier and better for the teacher to correct this problem before the student gets so far behind that failure is almost certain. To be in a position to take early action, you must collect and check student work frequently and also maintain good records. When you note a student who has begun to miss assignments, you can talk with him or her, seeking further information to help identify the problem, and then take corrective action. If the student is simply unable to do the assigned work, you should provide appropriate assistance or modify the assignments for that student. If the student feels overwhelmed by the assignments, break them up into parts whenever possible. Have the student complete the first part of the assignment within a specific time (perhaps five or ten minutes), then check to see that it has been done. A bonus of a few minutes of free time at the end of the period can be offered for completion of the portion within the time limit or for working steadily without prodding. Sometimes you can provide a list of assignments for the student to check off. This can serve as a self-monitoring device and can provide a sense of accomplishment.

If ability is not the problem, then in addition to talking with the student, the following procedures can be used. Call the student's parents and discuss the situation with them. Often the home can supply the extra support needed to help motivate the student. A simple penalty of requiring that the student remain after school until assignments have been completed can prove effective. If the student rides a bus, you won't be able to use the procedure, of course, without making special arrangements with the parents. Any time the child is likely to be detained for more than a few minutes, you should alert the parents ahead of time. Another procedure that can be used when the parents are cooperative is for the child to take home daily a list of incomplete assignments and all books or materials needed to complete the work.

Be sure not to soften the negative consequences of repeated failure to complete work by giving the students higher grades than they have earned. To do so just teaches them to avoid responsibility. Finally, try to provide added incentives for good effort and completed work. Set up a reward system (see Chapter 6) that encourages the children to do their best.

Fighting

Fighting is less likely to occur in classrooms than on the playground, in the cafeteria, or in some other area of the school. In the elementary grades you can usually stop a fight without undue risk of injury. (If for some reason you cannot intervene directly, you should of course alert other teachers and administrators so that action can be taken.) When you do intervene, first give a loud verbal command to stop. This alone may stop the fight; it will at least alert the combatants that a referee has arrived. Then separate the fighters. Keep them apart until help arrives, and get them away from the crowd that's sure to have gathered.

Your school will undoubtedly have a procedure to deal with fighting; you should carry it out. Students may be questioned by the principal, who may call the student's home, arrange a conference, and mete out any prescribed penalty.

If school policy leaves the teacher with wide discretion in following up on such incidents, then you should decide on your procedures. It is generally best to

© 1968 by Bill Knowlton. Reprinted from *Classroom Chuckles* published by Scholastic Book Services.

". . . and suddenly there were teachers all over the place!"

arrange a cooling-off period. If you cannot find someone to supervise your class, let the fighters wait in separate areas or in the school office. Older children can cool off by writing their version of how the fight started. If you do not know what started the fight, try to find out from uninvolved students. As soon as you have an opportunity, meet with the offenders and get each one's point of view. The conference should focus on the inappropriateness of fighting and the need to resolve problems in other ways rather than on accusations or personal criticism. Help each student understand the other's point of view so that they have a basis for better communication. Finally, stress the importance of cooperativeness and friendliness toward one another. During the next day or two watch for any indications of residual hostility. If the issue seems not to have been resolved, you should follow up by contacting the children's parents, discussing the matter with your principal, and/or talking with the students again.

Other Aggressive Behavior

Aggressive behavior toward other students is not confined to open fighting. Name calling, overbearing bossiness or rudeness toward other students, and physically aggressive but "playful" pushing, shoving, or slapping are examples of other forms of aggressive behavior found in the classroom. Such behavior should be treated just like rudeness toward the teacher. You should tell offending students that such behavior is not acceptable, even if they are just "fooling around." It can easily escalate. Refer to whatever class rule fits the situation, such as "Respect others." Give no more than one warning and then assess whatever penalty is appropriate. Students engaged in such behavior should be separated and seated apart if they give any indication of intending to persist.

Defiance or Hostility Toward the Teacher

Defiance or hostility is understandably very threatening to teachers. The teacher feels, and rightfully so, that if he or she allows the student to get away with it, the behavior may continue and other students will be more likely to react in the same way. The student who has provoked a confrontation, usually publicly, feels that backing down would cause a loss of face in front of peers. The best way to deal with such an event is to try to defuse it by keeping it private and handling it individually with the student, if possible. If it occurs during a lesson and is not very extreme, deal with it by trying to depersonalize the event and avoid a power struggle: "This is taking time away from the lesson. I will discuss it with you in a few minutes when I have time." If the student does not accept the opportunity you have provided and presses the confrontation further, then instruct the student to leave the room and wait in the hall. After the student has had time to cool off, give your class something to do and discuss the problem with the student.

When discussing the incident, you should remain objective. Remember—act, don't react. Do not engage in arguments with the student. Point out that the behavior was not acceptable, state the penalty clearly, and implement it. Listen to the student's point of view and respond to it. If you are not sure how to respond, say that you will think about it and discuss it later. However, you should still administer the penalty.

In an extreme (and rare) case, the student may be totally uncooperative and refuse to keep quiet or to leave the room. If this happens, you can escort the student from the room yourself or, when dealing with an older and/or larger student, send another student to the office for assistance. In most cases, however, as long as you stay calm and refuse to get into a power struggle with the student, the student will accept the opportunity to cool down.

A FINAL REMINDER: THINK AND ACT POSITIVELY

In this chapter, many of the strategies for dealing with problem behaviors involve some form of punishment. This is especially the case for the strategies in the moderate and extensive categories. A drawback to punishment is that, by itself, it doesn't teach the student what behaviors should be practiced. Consequently, it is important for teachers using one of these approaches also to communicate clearly about those behaviors that are desired. That is, the focus should remain on teaching appropriate behaviors. Furthermore, a classroom in which the main consequences are negative will not have a very good climate. Thus, teachers using strategies in the moderate and extensive categories more than occasionally should try to incorporate some additional incentives or a reward system into their overall classroom management to help mitigate the effects of using punishment. Finally, after correcting children's behavior, the teacher who supplies a generous helping of warmth and affection will reassure them that they have been restored to good grace.

SUGGESTED ACTIVITIES

1. Review the descriptions of problem types presented at the beginning of the chapter. Then decide which interventions would be best suited for each type. Given several alternative interventions for any type of problem, how would you decide which to use?

2. Within each type of intervention—minor, moderate, or extensive—are there any that you distinctly prefer? Do you reject any? Discuss your reasons for liking or disliking particular approaches.

3. Listed below are several problem behaviors. Decide on a strategy for dealing with each and also an alternative response if your first approach does not produce good results. Indicate any assumptions you are making about the teaching context as you choose your strategy.

■ *Situation 1.* Ardyth and Melissa talk and pass notes as you conduct a class discussion. Several other students whisper or daydream.

■ *Situation 2.* Desi and Bryce talk constantly. They refuse to get to work and argue with you when you ask them to open their books.

■ *Situation 3.* Joe manages to get most of his work done, but in the process he is constantly disruptive. He teases the girls sitting around him, keeping them constantly laughing and competing for his attention. Joe makes wisecracks in response to almost anything you say. When confronted, he grins charmingly and responds with exaggerated courtesy, much to the delight of the rest of the class.

■ *Situation 4.* When someone bumped into Marc at the drinking fountain, he turned around and spit water at the other child. Later, Marc ordered a boy who was standing near his desk to get away, and he then shoved the boy. On the way back from the cafeteria, Marc got into a name-calling contest with another boy.

Managing
Special Groups

Although the classroom management principles and guidelines discussed in previous chapters of this book apply to most classroom settings, classroom management is also affected by the characteristics of students making up the class. The ages, academic ability levels, goals, interests, and home backgrounds of students have an impact on their classroom behavior. Consequently, adjustments in management and instructional organization practices are sometimes needed to meet the needs of different groups of students. Among the students that frequently present some special challenges are students who are working below or well above grade level, students who are academically or physically handicapped, and students whose English language skills are limited. Often a classroom includes all of these types of students, which presents a special challenge to a teacher. Meeting the needs of students with such diverse needs and abilities requires special effort. Since individual learning rates are natural and acceptable, activities should promote acceptance of these facts and make helping and interacting natural and productive. This chapter presents some information and suggestions that, combined with the principles in previous chapters, will help you organize and manage classes with a range of student achievement or ability levels, groups of students with below level skills, and students with special needs in the classroom.

ASSESSING ENTERING ACHIEVEMENT

To identify the extent of differences in needs and ability levels (i.e., the degree of heterogeneity) in your classroom, you should use several sources of information. These sources include tests you administer, your own observation of each child, and indicators of performance available in each child's file, including assessments obtained from prior teachers and standardized achievement test information. Of course, if you have a student identified as a special needs student, you will consult with the resource teacher. Be cautious about forming a hasty impression of a child's abilities based on only one source of information. Furthermore, you must guard against the possibility of forming a negative self-fulfilling prophecy—forming low expectations of some students and communicating these to students, causing them to achieve below their potential.

Because of the importance of reading, language arts, and mathematics skills in the elementary school curriculum, these subjects will be the major focus of your initial assessment. As you evaluate your students, you should also be alert to indicators of study and work habits, such as the ability to follow directions and to maintain attention to a task. Children with very poor skills or who are highly distractible may require special consideration in your room arrangement, in planning for instructional activities, and in monitoring.

When obtaining information about entering reading and math skill levels, special attention must be given to those students for whom you lack information. Typically, these will be students who have transferred from another school district. You must also be careful about the assessment of children for whom existing information is not consistent. It is especially important to assess such children individually by listening to them read and checking their vocabulary and word attack skills and by testing to identify their math skills. You should consult with other teachers and/or other professionals for help in selecting suitable assessment procedures if you do not already have them.

It is best to delay individual student assessment until several days after the beginning of school. During such testing it will be difficult for you to monitor your class, and you may also have to leave students too long in seatwork. By delaying testing, you will also have a chance to observe the students first, and the students will become better acquainted and more comfortable with you before they are tested. If you do individual testing, plan enough work to keep your class busy. When several students need to be assessed individually, space the testing over several days.

© 1968 by Bill Knowlton. Reprinted from *Classroom Chuckles* published by Scholastic Book Services.

"I'm an underachiever. . . .
What's *your* racket?"

IDENTIFYING SPECIAL GROUPS

For the purpose of classroom instruction, it is important to determine the range of entering achievement in basic skill subjects, the degree to which individual students are unable to work effectively with the grade-level curriculum, and other special needs of your students. Other characteristics, such as student interests and backgrounds, can also affect learning and instruction and should be considered whenever possible as you plan instructional activities and set goals.

Information on student ability levels can be used to identify small groups for instruction, to pair students for peer tutoring, or to create cooperative groups for learning activities. Each of these types of activities requires special planning and management considerations.

STRATEGIES FOR INDIVIDUAL DIFFERENCES

In the next sections we will describe some strategies frequently used to adjust for individual differences and examine management concerns associated with these.

Team Teaching

Teachers at the same grade level frequently form teams to deal with heterogeneous student populations. Some students can then be reassigned to different teachers on the team for instruction in one or more subjects. This allows teachers to form relatively more homogeneous subgroups than would be possible using only students initially assigned to their individual classrooms. For example, two or three students whose entering reading skills are extremely low might be grouped for reading instruction with similar students from other classrooms. At the same time students at the highest level in the classes might be combined into a single group and taught by another teacher on the team. This arrangement permits instruction for these students to be targeted closer to their skill levels than if the students remained in their original classes. Still it is important that these students also participate in groups with mixed ability levels in some activities.

Team approaches to student heterogeneity can be applied to a variety of subjects but are most common in reading and mathematics instruction. Teaming should be considered whenever the range of student ability is too great to be accommodated by three groups in reading and by two groups in mathematics. Although extreme heterogeneity within a class could theoretically be accommodated by forming more groups, to do so is usually not practical because it would place excessive demands on teacher planning and would reduce the amount of time each group receives for instruction. Because teaming requires careful planning and cooperation, the following items are important to consider.

Coordination of Schedules

The teachers on the team must establish compatible schedules for the subjects being team taught. If teachers deviate from the schedule without warning, children from other classrooms may be kept waiting with nothing to do, and everyone will be thrown off schedule.

Student Movement

Because some students will be going from one room to another, they must be taught what procedures and behavior to use during transitions. A teacher should accompany children in transit between rooms, at least until they have learned the routine.

Reminding Students What They Are Supposed to Take with Them

Sometimes children have trouble remembering their materials. When they do not bring the appropriate materials, they may be sent back to their classrooms, losing valuable instructional time and sometimes disturbing students in both rooms. If students will need different sets of materials on different days, all teachers involved should be notified so they can help students remember what will be needed and when, perhaps by posting a list of materials to take or by reminding students as they prepare to leave the room.

Rules and Procedures

Students coming to you from another teacher's class will not know your expectations for their behavior. Therefore, you will need to discuss rules for conduct in your room and the procedures needed for small-group work and seatwork. Do this when you first meet with your new students. Then monitor them carefully until good behavior becomes established. If possible, plan rules and procedures with other members of the team in order to establish a common set of expectations. Consistency across settings will simplify the task of teaching students to behave correctly.

Maintaining Responsibility for Work

In addition to rules for conduct and procedures for behavior, care must be taken to keep students responsible for their work. This may be harder to do in a team-teaching situation than with the students in your regular class because the full range of incentives, penalties, and parental contact may be limited. Also, you will not be able to supervise the students at other times of the day when they might have an opportunity to work on assignments (and when, ideally, you would check work and provide supplementary instruction). For these reasons, several steps should be followed to keep students accountable:

1. Be certain that students, especially younger children, realize that you are responsible for checking their work and assigning a report card grade.

2. Be clear about your expectations for work, other requirements, and your grading criteria.

3. When you meet with students each day, check their work before you dismiss them, and give students whatever feedback they will need to complete the work successfully.

4. Return graded papers promptly. Don't let these materials accumulate.

5. Contact parents if children begin to skip assignments in your class. Don't rely on the homeroom teacher to do this.

Modifying Whole-Class Instruction

In some subjects the use of small groups for instruction will not be feasible or even desirable. Limited time, the problem of ascertaining individual differences on relevant entering skills, and greater procedural complexity may make small-group instruction less efficient than whole-class instruction. When used for subjects such as science or social studies, whole-class instruction can be modified to accommodate extremes in student abilities and interests. A number of simple modifications and cautions should be considered.

Interactive Instruction

You should try to involve all the students in presentations, discussions, and recitations. Do so by making a conscious effort to call on all students, not just those who are eager to respond. Students with a special ability or an obvious interest in a topic can be encouraged to complete special projects and to organize their ideas in oral reports to the class. These opportunities will allow the students to advance their understanding and receive recognition.

Seating Arrangements

Students who need closer supervision or more than the usual amount of explanation should be seated near the front of the room (or wherever you usually conduct whole-class presentations). Their proximity to you will enable you to check for understanding more readily and make it easier to monitor their behavior and progress.

Directions

Communicating instructions and directions to a highly diverse class requires care. Be certain you have all students' attention and provide both oral and written directions when feasible. Some students have difficulty following a long series of verbal directions. Break directions into student-manageable chunks and provide visual cues. The use of questions to verify comprehension and careful monitoring will also be helpful. Be certain to check with those students who frequently have problems following directions. If you have seated them near you, then you will be able to provide them with added assistance as needed.

Assignments

If you give the same assignments to all the students in a highly heterogeneous class, the work may be much too easy for some students and much too difficult for others. Consider giving assignments in two parts: a basic assignment for all students to complete and a second, more difficult part that is assigned to some students or that can be completed for extra credit. When assignments are the same for everyone, the students will complete them with different degrees of proficiency and speed. In such cases, use a grading or credit system that, at least in part, emphasizes individual student progress rather than competition among students. Enrichment or extra-credit material for students who finish classwork early should be work-related and should not distract other students. Avoid free-time activities that are so attractive that slower working students feel deprived or attempt to quit or rush through their work. Set up a system for giving credit, feedback, or recognition for completion of enrichment activities. If you allow students to read when they finish work, be sure to provide supplementary reading materials at a variety of reading levels.

Supplementary (Pull-out) Instruction

Sometimes students' needs in some subject areas cannot be well met in a regular classroom. For example, a child's skills may be so deficient in reading or math that he or she cannot profit from small-group instruction; even the lowest group may be too far beyond the child's current level. Or a child may be so distracted by the stimulation of twenty-five or thirty students in a regular classroom that he or she cannot focus on assignments long enough to complete them. Such children may fall behind in their performance, even though they possess average or above-average ability. Children whose first language is not English may need intensive help that cannot be provided in the regular instructional program. Finally, some children may possess special talents that programs for the gifted can more fully develop. In all of these cases supplementary programs may be available. The term *pull-out* is sometimes applied to these programs because the children are taken out of the regular classroom for part of the school day in order to receive special instruction. You will need to check to see if a student is enrolled in a pull-out program that is intended to supplement or to replace his or her regular classroom instruction. This will have important implications for your planning. Examples of pull-out programs include the following:

- Special education: This is usually available in a resource room. Children with learning disabilities and other conditions that interfere with learning or adjustment in a regular classroom setting receive instruction (usually reading and/or math) for part of the day. These children return to the regular classroom for other instruction.
- Chapter I programs: These are special programs established in schools that serve children from lower-income families. Students with deficits in academic skills receive supplementary instruction from special teachers.
- Enrichment programs: Programs that provide enrichment in particular subjects are often established for students who have special talent in the area. These programs frequently use community resources, parents, or other volunteers as well as the regular teaching staff to provide programs during school hours or after hours.

The aspect of supplementary programs that has a major impact on your classroom management plan will be the removal of students from your classroom during the time that regular instruction is proceeding. Thus, scheduling must be carefully planned so that the pull-out students do not miss essential instruction and so that the other students' instructional program is not interrupted. Transitions out of and back into your classroom also can become a major headache if they are not handled well.

Coordinating Times with Other Teachers

As soon as schoolwide schedules are set for lunch periods and activities such as music, art, and physical education classes, plan a schedule with the other teachers that will be as convenient as possible for everyone. If a number of students leave for special reading instruction, try to arrange with the reading teacher to have these students leave in a group at a time when you will be meeting with a reading group in your class. If several students will be pulled out for special instruction in a subject such as mathematics, you will probably want to schedule your math instruction for the rest of the class at that time.

Staying on Schedule

When class schedules involve pull-outs and drop-ins, it is especially important for teachers to stay on schedule so that students can be where they need to be at appropriate times. Have a large clock placed where everyone can see it. If you have trouble remembering to look at the clock, enlist the aid of the students in prompting you. Older students should eventually assume responsibility for their own schedules. You may want to post a list of times when different students are supposed to leave, in order to remind both you and the students. You can also set a timer as a reminder.

Having Something for Drop-in Students To Do While Waiting for Instruction

Sometimes a teacher is not quite through with one group when it is time for another group to meet. Students who are working at their desks in the teacher's room should have enough activities to keep them busy. However, drop-in students sometimes arrive early and have nowhere specific to sit, other than in the small group. You will need a procedure for dealing with these students so that small groups and seatworkers are not distracted. Some teachers tell students to take an empty seat while waiting. Other teachers set aside a waiting area on a small rug or at a table. While there, students can get a copy of their textbook or workbook and begin reading the next lesson or do other constructive activities.

Getting Returning Students Involved Again

After receiving instruction outside the room, some pull-out students may tend to dawdle or seem confused about what they are supposed to do when they return to the room. The best way to avoid confusion is to establish routines so that students always know what to do when they return. It is a good idea to post assignments or give students a list of assignments to help them remember. If you are working with a small group when some students return, give the small group something to do and go to the returning students to be sure they get back on task. Student helpers could also be given the responsibility for explaining the assignment or activity to individual returning students.

Activities when Supplementary Instruction Is Not Held

Sometimes the special teacher will be absent or the special class will not be conducted for some other reason. When this occurs it is important to have something for these students to do while you carry on with regular instruction. In some cases students may be included in regular class activities. In other cases you will have to provide special activities. If possible, meet regularly with the other teachers so that you will know what students are working on and be able to assign appropriate tasks. Try to have some free-time or enrichment activities set aside to accommodate varying levels of ability. It is important to monitor these students and give them something meaningful to do; otherwise, they may become bored or disruptive.

In-Class Aides

Sometimes teachers are fortunate enough to have parents or other adult volunteers, teacher aides, or university education students to help out in their classrooms. These aides may be assigned to help with a particular subject or be available to help with any subjects. Other aides may help with materials and administrative tasks and have little contact with the children. If you have one or more aides, there are several things you will need to do to promote smooth functioning in your classroom. You should be specific in informing the aide of his or her responsibilities for teaching or working with students and for disciplining students. You will probably want aides to enforce your rules consistently when they are in charge of students. If you must leave the room, inform students that the aide will be in charge of the class and will enforce the rules as you do. If the aide will be working with individual students or small groups, you will need to make available a space that will not cause distractions for the rest of the class, particularly if you are instructing simultaneously. Students should be told whether and when they may go to the aide for help.

Individualized Instruction

When each student receives instruction, is given assignments at a level established by careful assessment of entering skills, and is encouraged to progress at whatever pace his or her abilities and motivation allow, then the instructional program is said to be individualized. Some educators consider individualized instruction to be the best means of coping with heterogeneity because it offers, at least in principle, instruction tailored to the needs of each child. However, individualized instruction is difficult to implement. It requires (1) careful and continuous assessment of individual pupil progress, (2) management of time so that all students receive adequate interactive instruction from the teacher, (3) sufficient resources, including materials suitable for all ability levels in the class, and (4) the time for the teacher to plan and develop appropriate activities. The absence of one or more of these features will make it difficult to mount an effective instructional program. Also, teachers who wish to implement such programs should do so gradually, allowing themselves adequate time to develop the necessary resources. Because of these difficulties, we regard the first lines of defense for coping with heterogeneity and low-achieving students to be the modification of whole-class instruction, supplementary instruction, and team teaching. Only when these strategies are not adequate should individualized instruction be necessary.

When individualization of instruction is used for one or more subjects, you should anticipate a number of management problems and take action to prevent them or at least minimize their impact.

Transitions

Students engaged in individual rather than group activities will generally end them at different times. If the next activity is also an individual activity, then many individual transitions will occur throughout the period of instruction. This can cause much confusion and lost time. Some students may not know what to do; others may delay starting the next activity. More efficient transitions can be effected if the teacher is alert to help students who are between activities. Assignments must be posted or written somewhere so that students will know what to do next. The teacher can also have students bring completed work to be checked in order to provide some structure during the transition and to be certain that students know how to get started on the next activity.

Student Movement

Movement between locations of activities is more difficult to manage when students complete or start them at varying times. Because the teacher is frequently working with one or a few students at a time, less supervision of movement is possible, and students may begin to wander around frequently, wasting time and distracting other students. Student movement should be regulated by procedures that make clear when and for what purpose students may move around, converse with other students, or be out of their seats. Identifying the reason for excessive wandering or out-of-seat behavior can be helpful in remedying it. If students have completed their work satisfactorily and have nothing to do, then more challenging work or enrichment is appropriate. If students quit working because they are not able to do the assignment, then additional instruction, assistance, or modified assignments are in order.

Monitoring Student Behavior

Different expectations for students in different activities, along with a variety of simultaneous activities, make monitoring student behavior during individualized instruction difficult. Also, the teacher often instructs individual students or performs other tasks associated with individualized instruction (such as assessment), thus adding to the complexity of monitoring. To overcome these problems, the following key behaviors should be practiced:

- Know what all students are supposed to be doing at any given time so that you can support their efforts and prevent problems.

- Be sure students know what they are expected to do and what conduct is appropriate in different activities.

- Be alert for students who are having difficulty getting started or completing an activity, so that you can provide help. Don't get overly engrossed with helping one or a few students, and don't wait until students quit working or become disruptive before providing assistance.

- Circulate among the students and look at their work periodically. Scan the room frequently to detect early signs of frustration or task avoidance.

- Usually a few students will require more supervision than others. When possible, be sure these students are seated where you can observe and assist them readily.

Encouraging Student Responsibility for Work

The use of an individualized instruction program does not guarantee that students will accept responsibility for completing assignments and participating in learning activities. In fact, some students will take advantage of the more complex instructional arrangements and limitations on the teacher's monitoring capability to avoid responsibility and to expend minimal effort. To avoid these problems, you must give clear directions for assignments and other activities.

Many teachers prefer to review directions with students at the beginning of the period devoted to the individualized instructional activities. A basic set of activities can often be listed on the chalkboard and reviewed, or students can be given activity or assignment folders that list what is to be done. Such a folder can also be used to check off completed work. This system helps both the teacher and the students keep track of progress. Setting time limits for work on one activity before proceeding to the next will help students pace their efforts.

Students should expect their work to be checked frequently. If they get accustomed to simply completing one activity and starting a new one without feedback, their performance will deteriorate. The teacher should develop monitoring procedures that include periodic progress checks and evaluation and feedback on completed assignments and other work. It is also important to review overall student progress and decide whether the pace and scope of work are adequate. Some teachers prefer weekly or biweekly reviews and a short conference with individual students for this purpose.

Sometimes the teacher's role in individualization diminishes to the point where almost all the teacher's time is devoted to making assessments, giving assignments, keeping records, and checking. When this occurs, students receive little interactive instruction from the teacher and do little except complete worksheets. The teacher's diminished instructional role may be partly due to the incorrect perception that because instruction is individualized, the teacher can only instruct one student at a time. In fact, it is far more efficient if the teacher presents information and conducts recitations with groups of students, supplementing these group lessons with individual instruction for students who require extra help.

Contracts

These are often used with individual instruction. Contracts usually include a list of assignments or activities to be completed by a student during a fixed period of time, such as a day or a week. Contracts also may specify the goals or objectives, materials, and incentives associated with completing the contract. Use of a contract has a number of advantages. It is a good way to communicate assignments and objectives, it enables students to suggest modifications that they would find helpful or interesting, and the student's signature on the contract can increase motivation for completion within the agreed-upon time period.

Student Cooperation: Help from Peers

Another method for coping with extreme heterogeneity and for dealing with low achievers is to use students to help other students. Examples of such peer helping arrangements include the following:

- Students work in pairs, reading and listening to each other read. "Reading with a buddy" can be part of contract work.
- Certain students are assigned as monitors to help other students when the teacher is busy with group or individual instruction.
- When the teacher is busy with small-group instruction, students who need help are encouraged to get assistance from another student before interrupting the teacher.
- Group leaders are assigned to each learning station to answer questions and to set up materials.
- A capable, mature student is assigned as a helper for another student who needs frequent assistance. The helper's responsibilities are to answer questions and explain directions.
- Students may be permitted to help or seek help from a neighbor on some seatwork activities.

When using students as helpers, you should recognize the potential for excessive noise, poor attention to the task, or excessive reliance on the helper by the helpee. Also, not all students are amenable to this type of arrangement or work well together. These negative effects can be averted by communicating clearly what is and is not permitted and by monitoring the helping arrangements and relationships to be sure no undesirable side effects develop. As is true for all of the variations from regular instruction patterns, gradual introduction of new arrangements will give the best opportunity for managing their implementation and for correcting problems.

Cooperative Work Groups

For many activities, using small groups with mixed-ability levels and/or diverse backgrounds provides a good opportunity for all students to help and to learn from each other. Researchers such as Robert Slavin (1990) have shown that working in mixed-ability teams can benefit both higher and lower achieving students in many subject areas. Benefits of cooperative groups include increased student achievement, positive race relations, mutual concern among students, and increased student self-esteem.

Effective use of cooperative student groups requires several components: mixed-ability (or background) groups, a reward structure that provides for individual as well as group rewards, and well-chosen activities. The selection of appropriate cooperative groups entails careful assignment of students to groups or teams rather than just letting students choose their friends and assignment of student roles within the groups to ensure that all students play active roles. Most of the cooperative group designs call for a mixture of high achieving (or high ability), average achieving, and lower achieving students or students with special needs. In some types of cooperative group activities, each student is expected to learn or be responsible for a certain amount of lesson content, to instruct the rest of the group in that content, and to learn from the rest of the group members the content for which they are responsible. In other types of cooperative group activities the groups work together to complete a task and ensure that all group members have learned the content. Each member of the group is required to participate.

An essential component of cooperative groups is the reward structure. An effective reward structure typically includes a combination of individual and group rewards. Each individual in the group must feel that his or her performance will be rewarded individually for effort and performance, compared against others of similar levels. In addition, rewarding the group's performance encourages the interaction of group members working toward a common purpose.

The use of cooperative groups entails a number of management considerations. Guidelines for structuring and managing small-group work are included in Chapters 2 and 5. Issues related to selection of and record keeping for rewards are addressed in Chapter 6.

Peer Tutoring

Peer tutoring provides an opportunity for each student to have access to one-on-one assistance, particularly when the teacher is unavailable to provide assistance. This can be done during class by pairing students at similar levels to work together or by asking a student who has achieved a certain level or learned a concept to work with another student who has not. The student who receives assistance benefits from individualized instruction. The helper, or peer tutor, benefits from planning for and explaining the concept.

To use peer tutoring effectively, certain management issues must be addressed. You must decide when tutoring is and is not acceptable. There may be some subjects for which peer tutoring is not appropriate. For instance, you may not be assured that the potential peer tutors have sufficiently learned the concept to be able to provide assistance.

You will also want to decide where tutoring will occur. Some teachers provide a special location within the classroom where peer interactions are less likely to interrupt other classroom activities or disturb students who are working unassisted. Others may allow students to work quietly side-by-side at their desks.

If you are going to use peer tutors, it is a good idea to train students to be peer tutors. Potential peer tutors should be shown how to model behaviors, instructed in how to ask questions to assess the other student's understanding, and counseled on interpersonal behaviors. For long-term peer tutors, you may want to provide a brief training during class or after school. Other directions can be given as part of the overall instructions for an activity.

WORKING WITH SPECIAL NEEDS STUDENTS

This section deals with students who have special needs, either because they are physically or mentally handicapped or because they have background characteristics that affect their classroom performance, such as language proficiency.

Recent research on students with special needs because of physical or mental handicaps has shown the benefits of providing instruction to these students in the least restrictive environment. As a result, more and more students with special needs are being served in the regular classroom with some outside help from specialized teachers. Meeting these students' needs presents special challenges to teachers with a classroom full of children. Fortunately, research has provided some specific guidelines to help teachers work with these students in ways that promote their peer acceptance and their self-esteem as well as their academic achievement. Following are some suggestions for planning instruction for children with different types of special needs.

Learning Disabled Students

Although there is still no consensus as to a concise definition of learning disability, certain characteristics are commonly seen. A primary feature is more difficulty with and lower achievement in certain academic areas than would otherwise be expected based on these students' overall ability levels. Other common problems experienced by these students are disorganization and a disconcerting tendency to forget something they seemed to understand thoroughly just a short time earlier. Accompanying these difficulties is a natural sense of frustration and the risk of developing a generalized attitude of anger or hopelessness along with a negative view of themselves.

Learning disabled students generally respond well to a positive and structured approach, with predictable routines. They may forget steps in even familiar routines, however, and require much patience and repetition. These students need more help than others in learning to identify and pay attention to relevant cues. Point out cues and relevant directions, and have students repeat directions out loud to be sure they understand what to do. Place a special emphasis on what is correct, rather than on what they are doing wrong. Model the appropriate behavior or actions to ensure they are transferring positive learning rather than reinforcing negative learning. Avoid trial and error activities where they may spend too much time doing the wrong thing, thus adding to their confusion.

Overlearning is important for these students, especially because of their retention problems. Remember it is more helpful to distribute numerous short practices of tasks over a period of time than to have fewer long practices. These children benefit from a wide range of multisensory experiences in learning concepts. These experiences help learning disabled children to overcome problems they have due to lack of experience with their environments. Be aware that although social praise may help motivate, it may also interfere with development of independent decision-making skills. Use praise sparingly, gradually reducing it to enhance internal motivation and satisfaction.

Learning disabled children often develop behavior problems. They may benefit from keeping their own record of specific behaviors, including completion of assignments. This helps them to build a sense of control over themselves and their environment.

Emotionally Disturbed Students

Remembering that emotionally disturbed children are usually different from others merely in the degree of emotionality rather than in the type of feelings they have may relieve some potential anxiety in working with these students. Be sure to read the psychological report describing these children and note any recommendations made. Consult with the school psychologist and special education teacher about ways of working with your emotionally disturbed student. If these are children who have temper outbursts or become easily frustrated and angry, reinforce all attempts they make toward self-control. Learn to recognize any behavioral cues that may precede an outburst so you may anticipate and intervene to prevent their losing control. Overlook minor inappropriate behavior, reinforce acceptable behavior, and reduce stressors, including lowering expectations temporarily if the student is having a bad day. Provide a supportive, predictable environment, offering the students structured choices when possible (e.g., Would you prefer to do the odd numbered problems or the even numbered? or, Would it be helpful for you to work awhile in the study carrel or do you think you can concentrate well enough at your own desk?).

Work with your principal, counselor, and other teachers to devise a plan to carry out if your emotionally disturbed students have a tantrum or blow up. They may need to be removed from the classroom (or have the other students removed) to allow them to be separate from other children for awhile. A safe time-out area should be designated for this purpose, and they should continue to be supervised as they cool down. Remember that these students often do not know why they lose control, although as they get older they will tend to blame something or someone outside themselves. They do not generally understand how their feelings relate to what has happened, and afterwards they are often embarrassed and remorseful. It is important to reestablish your relationship with them once you and they are again calm. Other than attempting to learn from each incident in an effort to prevent future occurrences, let each incident be forgotten and do not remind the students of past failures.

It is crucial that you not take their lack of cooperation, inappropriate behavior, or verbal attacks personally. Should they lash out at you, remember that you are merely the convenient target, not the root cause of their pain and/or rage.

Attention-Deficit Hyperactive Disorder Students

Broad characteristics of these children's behavior include distractibility, a short attention span, impulsiveness, an inability to organize, and a high level of movement. Annoying as these behaviors are, it is important to remember that they are not deliberate and that it is very difficult and takes a long time for these children to learn ways to compensate for or control them. A low-key approach with much predictability and structure is almost essential to enable these students to function successfully. Talk with their parents to find out what kinds of things work at home, so home and school techniques will be compatible.

When giving oral instructions, be sure you have these children's attention. Give them brief and clear instructions, preferably one at a time. If a series of steps are involved, have them written in order and teach these children to complete one step before going on to the next. Closely monitor them as they begin any new assignment or activity, and be willing to state directions again individually. Adjust the amount of work required of these students within a time period compatible with their attention span. The amount may gradually be increased as their ability to concentrate increases. Remind these students that accuracy is more important than speed and that they need not be the first ones to speak up or to hand in assignments. Be willing to go pick up a completed assignment from these students, since they often lose completed work before turning it in. Let the students use cards with windows cut in them as a frame to help focus their attention on a specific area, problem, line of print, or paragraph. Teach them to use their fingers as pointers so they do not skip words or lines.

Organize the daily schedule so that stimulating or exciting activities come after, rather than before, activities requiring extended concentration. Allow these children to move around every few minutes, for example, to bring their paper to you after they have done a few parts of the assignment, such as a few math problems. Have available a spot that is relatively free of distractions and offer them the option of doing some of their work there. Prepare several low-pressure, fun activities for times when they need to spend a few minutes regaining control or relaxing. Teach them some relaxation techniques such as deep breathing, tensing and relaxing muscles, etc., to use during long work periods or tests to relieve tension. If the students receive medication at school, establish a cue or routine to help them remember to go to the nurse at the proper time. Monitor this until the students have assumed the responsibility successfully.

Hearing Impaired Students

Students with a serious hearing loss may be able to function well in regular classes with some minor but crucial modifications. Consult with a teacher specializing in auditory handicaps for techniques that might benefit your particular students. If assisting adaptive devices are available (e.g., FM auditory system, caption decoders for videos), use them. Seat these students near the center of the room and close to the front. Always face the students when speaking; use the overhead projector rather than the chalkboard as you talk so that they can see your face while you are writing. Have the room well-lighted so these students can clearly see your lips and face to lip-read. Do not stand in front of windows or a bright doorway while talking; the glare behind you will make your face difficult to see.

Often these students miss out on important information, being able only to catch portions of words or phrases. Remember that understanding is more complex than just hearing or responding to a name, and these students are often reluctant to ask you to repeat. Make it routine to repeat and rephrase important information or instructions and when possible, have it written as well. During class discussions, be sure to restate other students' questions and responses, since the hearing impaired students will probably not be able to lip-read these. Check frequently for understanding by asking these students a question during guided practice and closely monitoring as they begin written work. If note taking is required, assign a good student with legible handwriting who is willing to take notes using carbon paper or provide a copy to the hearing impaired student. This is especially important during films. Hearing impaired students cannot take notes and lip-read at the same time. You can also assign a buddy to cue the hearing impaired student when it is important to watch the teacher, to locate information in the text under discussion, and so on.

Students with Limited English Proficiency

There are many students in our schools for whom English is not their first language. Some of these students have acquired sufficient English language skills to perform successfully in English-only classes. Other students have not acquired a sufficient level of skill speaking, understanding, reading, or writing English, and need additional assistance to participate successfully in school activities.

Some schools provide bilingual classes where school content is presented in the native language and the student is provided assistance in learning English.

Other schools provide English as a Second Language (ESL) classes, geared toward helping the student learn English as quickly as possible so that content learning can proceed in English. For many students, English learning occurs in conjunction with content learning in a regular classroom, sometimes with the aid of a language teacher or aide.

While children who speak virtually no English will probably have a bilingual or an ESL teacher for most of the day, you may have several students who speak little English or you may have some of the non-English speaking students for part of the day. Find out from the bilingual or ESL teacher which children can understand some English and which ones understand none, so your expectations will be fair and realistic. Learn some key words in the child's native language from the bilingual or ESL teacher (or someone who speaks the language), such as "listen," "pay attention," "look," etc. Also learn what the children prefer to be called, and be sure to pronounce their names correctly. Rather than relying on someone to translate for you, use your creativity in communicating, speaking naturally and using pauses and many gestures. Reinforce key points with visual aids and demonstration when possible and by repeating them in clear and concise words. Because these children are used to tuning out English assuming they will not understand, ask the bilingual or ESL teacher to encourage them to pay close attention when they are with you to see if there are words or phrases they can understand or learn. Consider assigning peer "buddies," who are outgoing and warm, to communicate what you cannot, and to let you know if the children need your help even if they are reluctant to speak. A long receptive period is normal for students with limited proficiency in English during which they will respond with gestures, nods, etc., before they feel confident enough to speak any English words.

TEACHING LOWER ACHIEVING STUDENTS

Many teachers feel they need help in organizing instruction to successfully teach students who are on a low academic level. Whether you have a class with only a few low achievers or one with many children whose entering skills are far below grade level, you will need to give some special attention to the instructional needs of these students.

In many cases students who are achieving substantially below grade level come from disadvantaged or low socioeconomic status backgrounds. Research has shown that these students may not benefit from the same teaching strategies that work with average or high-achieving students who have learned how to learn early in life. In addition, some techniques that are good instructional practices with all student populations are especially important when teaching low-achieving students.

Active Instruction

Research has shown that students at a low academic level make more progress in basic skills when their teachers provide structured classroom activities with close teacher supervision and lots of active, teacher-led instruction. Large amounts of class time spent in unstructured or free-time activities should be avoided, as should situations calling for frequent student self-direction and self-pacing. It is especially important for lower achieving students to have many opportunities to interact with the teacher during instruction, and to answer teacher questions and receive feedback about their work. Low-achieving students should be seated where they can easily be monitored and given assistance.

Organizing and Pacing Instruction

When teaching lower achieving students, you can encourage more student learning and better classroom behavior if you break instruction into small segments or short activities with frequent assessments of student understanding. Avoid activity plans that require students to attend to a presentation or to work for twenty-five or thirty minutes at a stretch on the same seatwork assignment. Instead, use two or more shorter cycles of content development and work samples in each lesson, as described in Chapter 5. There are two distinct advantages of using several cycles instead of one when teaching lower ability students. One advantage is that it is easier to maintain student involvement. Also, by carefully monitoring the first seatwork/classwork exercise, you can easily observe whether students are able to complete the assignments, which in turn makes it easier for you to pace instruction appropriately and give ample feedback to students.

In planning lessons, keep in mind that especially with lower ability students it is better to cover material very thoroughly than to cover a lot of material quickly. Plan for plenty of practice and repetition, and keep your lesson plans flexible enough to allow for reteaching. This does not mean, however, that assignments for lower level students should be limited to routine, repetitious, and uninteresting work. On the contrary, assignments and class discussion should provide opportunities for all your students to think, be creative, and organize and apply what they know. At least some of the questions lower ability students encounter in written and oral work should give them practice with these higher level operations.

Plan introductions of new content very carefully. Clear communication is important in all classes, but it is especially important when teaching lower-achieving students. Careless, overly complex communication is likely to result in student confusion and frustration, and misbehavior. Follow the guidelines for clarity discussed in Chapter 7, paying careful attention to the amount of information presented at one time, appropriate vocabulary, and the use of concrete or specific examples to illustrate new concepts. Check for student understanding frequently. Avoid overlapping many procedural directions. Get students' attention, then present directions in a step-by-step fashion, waiting for students to complete each step before going on to the next.

Remedial Instruction

For learning to occur, all students (and especially lower achieving students) must be provided with instructional materials and tasks at which they can succeed. Lower achieving students often require remedial instruction. When beginning a new unit you may find that some students do not have prerequisite skills. Or after teaching a lesson you may realize that several students have not mastered the new skill. Both of these situations require that you provide remedial instruction. Two considerations are crucial: You must build time for remediation into your classroom activity plans, and you must get instructional materials that are appropriate for the students who need remediation. Talk with your instructional supervisor, a resource teacher, or other teachers to obtain instructional materials that your low-ability students will be able to complete successfully.

Building Positive Attitudes

Even in lower elementary grades, lower achieving students are more likely to have developed a poor self-image or poor attitude toward school. By the upper elementary grades lower academic level students have often fallen two or more grade levels below average for their grade and age group. Some may have failed one or more grades in previous years. Because of their frequent failure in school in the past, some of these students will have become very discouraged; they may react by giving up easily or by fighting back. These reactions may be evidenced in the extremes of apathy, shyness, belligerence, or clowning in class. Especially in earlier grades these students may perceive classroom events as arbitrary or mysterious. They do not expect to understand or to succeed in schoolwork, and maintaining their attention for long periods of time may be difficult, particularly when they encounter demanding or frustrating tasks.

As a teacher of lower achieving students, an important part of your task is to improve these students' self-images and expectations of accomplishment. There are several steps you can take. First, remember that it is important for these students to finish their work and not give up. This may require that you shorten assignments for some or provide students with extra time and encouragement to finish their work. Be careful, however, that the extra time lower achieving students are given to finish assignments does not prevent them from participating in interesting and worthwhile activities with the rest of the class. Constantly being denied participation in show-and-tell, art activities, interest centers, and recess will not contribute to an improved self-image. A better approach is to provide materials and assignments that lower achieving students are able to finish in the available time.

Class discussions are opportunities for students to display their knowledge. Because teachers' questions and students' answers are heard by everyone, the teacher's handling of discussions often communicates expectations about student performance. The way lower achieving students are treated during class discussions can have effects on their attitudes and achievement. Staying with students until they answer a question, giving them time to answer without being interrupted, providing constructive feedback to wrong answers, and helping students improve their answers are all ways that you can help low achieving students succeed.

A warm, supporting, and accepting classroom climate will benefit lower achieving students, but be thoughtful in your use of praise. Research suggests that praise is more helpful when it is specific and contingent on good work and/or good behavior. Don't make the mistake of frequently rewarding lower achieving students with vague or general praise, or praise for wrong answers or sloppy, incomplete work. This kind of teacher behavior may confuse students or convey the message that you don't expect much from them. Be alert for opportunities to give slower students deserved and specific praise.

WORKING WITH HIGHER ABILITY STUDENTS

Higher ability students may present special challenges in heterogeneous classes. The need to keep these students productively involved in learning activities requires that they be challenged at the appropriate level and be given sufficient activities to avoid boredom or disruption of the rest of the class.

Research has shown that higher ability students learn more when they are challenged. The level of success on activities can sometimes be lower than that needed for students with less ability; that is, they may not become as frustrated if they do not perform with an extremely high level of success. Effective teachers of higher ability students tend to work at a faster pace than normal with these students, and they introduce more variety in their teaching methods and materials.

It bears noting that not all of your high ability students will function in your classroom in the same way. Some high ability students may also be high achievers and these students are often a joy to work with. High achievers may be well-socialized, independent workers who have developed positive attitudes toward school and learning. Some high ability students, however, may appear very different. They may be highly creative, highly divergent, gifted thinkers who approach every problem you present in your classroom differently from their peers, or they may create behavior problems. You must be careful not to confuse compliant behavior with academic ability.

The ability, creativity, and divergence of gifted students should be nurtured and encouraged, but this may be difficult in a heterogeneous classroom. Classrooms with more open-ended assignments, where each student may pursue a project or a problem to the extent of his or her ability, may provide more support for divergent thinkers, and may help to avoid behavior problems which arise out of boredom or frustration with the limitations of highly structured assignments.

Have resource materials available for these students to use for bonus questions or extra projects. Develop a file box of index cards with a variety of ideas for projects. Include extra or bonus questions on all assignments and tests, and encourage these students to attempt these. If your classroom or school library has a computer, check out programs from your educational service center or public library that provide enrichment to areas you are covering in class. Involve these students in activities that can benefit others, such as peer tutoring, peer counseling, school improvement projects, etc. Encourage your higher ability students to keep up with current events (as appropriate for their age) and to write their questions or opinions to the newspaper or to people in the news.

Higher ability students can contribute greatly to the learning environment in your classroom. Their contributions to class discussions and activities may encourage creativity and divergent thought in your other students. Your response to them, as well as to the other special groups that will make up your class, will signal to all students whether or not their range of abilities, interests, and skills is welcomed and appreciated.

SUGGESTED ACTIVITIES

1. Read Case Study 9-1 to see one teacher's strategies for working with students with low reading levels.

2. Problems 9-1 and 9-2 describe two situations that elementary teachers frequently encounter. Use ideas presented in this chapter to identify some strategies that could be used in these situations. Check your ideas with the suggestions in the Appendix.

CASE STUDY 9-1

Organizing Reading Group Activities for Low Academic Level Students. Ms. Barstow had a group of boys who were very low achievers in reading and who had great difficulty in keeping themselves on-task. Rather than giving them independent assignments, as she could do with some others in the class, she arranged their reading activities so that she could give them small chunks of instruction and frequent feedback. She met with their reading group first. During instruction, she asked many questions with relatively short answers, calling on each child in the group in turn. She avoided letting any one student talk at length or wander from the academic question at hand. In this way she was able to keep everyone's attention focused on the work.

After carefully going over directions and checking students' comprehension of them, the teacher dismissed the group to perform a specific assignment at the listening center, where her voice on the prepared tape provided continuous direction. Later she met with them again briefly to check their work and to give them another short assignment. They were given about twenty minutes to work independently, and the teacher sat so that she could monitor them while she taught another group. After doing their seatwork assignment, they went to a Language Master machine (as previously directed by the teacher) to practice skills while the teacher worked with another group. Then the teacher quickly checked over the first group's and other children's work and ended the morning's reading group activities. Because the teacher had selected activities and arranged the schedule so that these boys did not have to depend on their own self-control for long periods of time, the boys were engaged in and attending to instructions or actively practicing skills for most of the morning.

PROBLEM 9-1

Team Teaching. Mr. Miller and two other fourth-grade teachers use team teaching for math instruction. Shortly after lunch each day, some students from the other teachers' classes come to Mr. Miller's room, while some of his students go to the other two teachers' rooms. Mr. Miller has grown dissatisfied with the arrangement because he feels that too much of his teaching time is wasted while groups change rooms, get organized, and get ready to work. Sometimes early-arriving students disrupt lessons. At other times, stragglers hold up the rest of the class. Students frequently arrive without the materials they need for that day. While Mr. Miller answers questions and deals with problems, students begin chatting and wandering around. When Mr. Miller is ready to start the lesson, he has trouble getting students settled down to work. What can Mr. Miller do to make teaming work more smoothly?

? PROBLEM 9-2

A Heterogeneous Class. Ms. Ortiz feels that her class this year is more difficult to teach than any she has had in her four years of teaching third grade. Of twenty-six students in class, seven are beginning the school year functioning at first-grade level or below in reading. Five of these seven are also far behind in mathematics concepts; the other two are on grade-level. Three students in the class have advanced reading and mathematics skills, while others are nearer to grade level. Ms. Ortiz is frustrated in her attempts to meet the needs of the slowest students while challenging the brighter students. She now conducts four reading groups. What strategies might Ms. Ortiz consider trying?

Appendix: Answer Keys for Chapter Activities

CHAPTER 1

Activity 1

The room arrangement shown in Figure 1-2 could contribute to classroom management problems in a number of ways:

- When the teacher presents information to the whole class from the area near the main chalkboard, students on the other side of the room will be quite distant from the chalkboard and the teacher. This will make it difficult for them to see some of the material written on the chalkboard, and it will be more difficult for the teacher to monitor these students. At the same time, the teacher's range of movement is restricted to a relatively small area, and there is no place to store materials needed in whole-group presentations.

- Traffic lanes are clogged or blocked, especially near the bookshelves and en route to the bathrooms and the pencil sharpener.

- The small-group tables in the center of the room are too near student desks. Not only might the arrangement cause distractions for students seated at their desks, but there is no place at the table where the teacher can sit and easily see everybody in the room.

- Because of the location of the bookcase, the center may be difficult to monitor.

- Some students have their backs to the chalkboard and to the main presentation area.

- When the teacher assists some individual students at their desks, he or she will have difficulty seeing students in several places in the room.

■ The isolated desk near the girls' restroom door is a source of potential problems. Not only does it block the path to the door, but a student seated at the desk would be distracted by and be a distraction to students coming and going from this area. Also, the location of the desk makes it very difficult for the teacher to monitor a student seated there.

■ The student sitting at the desk against the teacher's desk might be distracted if the teacher worked with other students at the desk. Also this desk is located far from the main instructional area.

CHAPTER 3

Case Study 3-4

Diagnosis. The continuing confusion of Mr. Ambrose's students about due dates, directions, and completion of work suggests that although he may have planned plenty of work for the students, he may not be explaining requirements clearly, nor checking for understanding frequently enough. In addition, students are not receiving feedback about their progress or the quality of their work, nor are there any apparent rewards or penalties connected with work completion or lack of it. Having students hold papers until the next day may result in many of them being misplaced and in further delay in receiving feedback about the correctness of the work.

Suggestions. Mr. Ambrose can begin to improve his situation by trying the following strategies:

■ Each assignment should be explained carefully and in detail in addition to being posted on the chalkboard. Students could also be encouraged to keep an assignment book or some other record of daily assignments in particular subjects. In addition, Mr. Ambrose could keep a record of the assignments in a folder so that students could refer to it if needed or check on assignments they missed while they were absent. Keeping several days' assignments posted on the chalkboard may be confusing unless these are clearly marked.

■ While giving directions and explanations, Mr. Ambrose should be aware of signs of confusion or inattention. He should also be sure to go over sample questions, problems, or exercises with the class, use a standard format for student headings on papers, and use routines whenever possible to avoid constantly having to reexplain or give new directions.

- Mr. Ambrose should also have students begin assignments under his direction. He can do a small part of the assignment orally, then question students to check their understanding until he is sure they can work independently.

- He should circulate around the class and monitor student progress rather than sit at his desk doing paper work. He should allow students to come to his desk for help only after they have tried the assignment. Then he should allow only one student at a time to come up. When several students need help, he should circulate around the class again, rather than encouraging "come-ups."

- Assignments should be checked and collected as they are completed. If they are too complex to be checked immediately, Mr. Ambrose should check for completeness and return incomplete work to the students to finish. It may be helpful to set aside one or two specific times each day to review each student's progress on their assignments. That way students will know they are accountable, and Mr. Ambrose can more easily identify problems that students are having with work. In addition he will be able to identify students who are having difficulty and need extra help before they get too far behind. Students who fail to turn in assignments should be given assistance and direction promptly.

- Students can be encouraged to set goals by helping them keep records of their scores on assignments in particular subjects. Mr. Ambrose may be able to boost motivation by encouraging the students to set a class goal of improved completion rates or overall student averages and may then provide a treat or a special activity as a reward.

CHAPTER 5

Problem 5-1

In organizing her students' day, Ms. Kendall must plan to accommodate both "school givens" of time and space and "pupil givens" of numbers and abilities. Before developing her daily schedule, Ms. Kendall must first check the school's master schedule to learn what times have been assigned to her class for lunch, recess, music, art, physical education, etc. In planning around these time constraints, she must consider how many students will be in the class, the range of their ability levels, and the size of the classroom. She must take into consideration both student attention patterns throughout the day and student attention spans within the day. As students tend to be more alert in the morning and less alert after lunch, she will want to schedule academic subjects accordingly.

Also, she will need to provide a variety of activities, with none lasting too long. Room size, however, will determine the number of centers and individual study areas available.

On the first day of school, Ms. Kendall's plans should include the following: greet the students; give a brief introduction of herself and her class; explain the areas of the room and procedures needed for the first week; begin a presentation and discussion of class rules, procedures, and consequences; direct a student get-acquainted activity; provide whole-class, uncomplicated academic activities; allow time to complete administrative tasks; have constructive "time fillers" ready for use if needed.

CHAPTER 5

Problem 5-2

The following suggestions for Mr. Hart could improve his students' seatwork performance:

- He should make sure everyone understands instructions before starting groups. Explanation alone may not be sufficient; students should be questioned and they should repeat key directions. Mr. Hart can also write the directions on the chalkboard. Students should be told what will be checked and when.

- If seatwork includes some silent reading, reading comprehension questions can be listed on the board so that students have a focus for their reading and know what they will be accountable for when they are called to the reading circle.

- Students may need help pacing themselves. The teacher can show them on the clock how much time the first assignment should take or set a timer to signal when they should be finished with a particular assignment.

- In order to have time to get the seatwork group started, Mr. Hart can give the first reading group a getting-ready task to complete before he joins them. This will enable him to monitor all seatwork students at the beginning of the activity to be sure they have made a good start.

- After working with the reading group for awhile, the teacher can give these students a short task to do on their own while he checks on the progress of out-of-group students and answers their questions. When out-of-group students are wasting time and in danger of not completing other necessary activities, their papers can be marked in red to show each student's progress on the first assignment. They can then start on their next assignment, but they should be required to finish the first assignment at home or later in class.

- Students should not be allowed to interrupt the teacher with questions during small-group instruction. Students should be told to skip troublesome parts until the teacher can talk to them, or student monitors can be assigned the responsibility of giving assistance to children who need it.

- A visual signal, such as a sign or a flag, can be used to inform students when they may approach the teacher with questions and when they may not.

- A "help" list for the class may be established. Children can sign the list if they want to talk to the teacher when he is busy. The teacher needs to be conscientious about checking the list and going to the children as soon as possible (e.g., between reading groups).

- Students need to know what they may and may not do once their assignments have been completed. They should be given free-time enrichment activities or provided with a good set of interesting materials for free reading.

CHAPTER 5

Problem 5-3

Apparently this type of instruction is new for Ms. Jackson's class, so students will need to learn a new set of procedures. They may be used to highly directed lessons, and they may not have had much science instruction. Ms. Jackson will need to explain the procedures for a discovery lesson, including how to work on your own and with a partner, and the purposes for this science lesson. She should make sure that she has everyone's attention before beginning the explanation. She should start by introducing the lesson and its purposes and demonstrating appropriate uses of the cups. She must make clear at the beginning what uses of the cups she sees as inappropriate.

Ms. Jackson must consider how to create a balance between overdirecting students and leaving them too much on their own. She should work through questions like those in Checklist 5 to focus on her purposes for this lesson and which aspects of it are new to her students. For example, what kind of product does she expect from her students? Will they demonstrate their findings, write a lab report, apply their findings to another situation? If pairs or groups work independently, what will they do if they finish at different times?

Ms. Jackson needs to develop a system for distributing and collecting materials, to minimize the time the teacher is unavailable to circulate and provide assistance. For example, she could appoint one student from each group as "Materials Manager" and set up a central place for that student to pick up cups for the group.

CHAPTER 5

Problem 5-4

See how many examples of Kounin's concepts you can find in the following description.

■ As he is about to begin class after lunch, Mr. Case makes eye contact with two students who are exchanging notes; the students quickly get out their class materials. (**Withitness.**) "Let's begin by working some of the exercises at the end of the chapter; you will need a piece of paper with a heading." As students begin to get out their materials, Mr. Case calls out, "Oops, I forgot to tell you to bring money for tomorrow for the field trip. How many of you will be going?" (**Thrust.**) After a brief discussion, students finish getting out their materials. Mr. Case says, "We'll go through these exercises orally, but I also want you to write the answers on your papers as part of today's classwork. I'll come around later and check your answers. (**High participation format and accountability.**) Now who can answer the first question? Hands please. Tyrone?" Mr. Case conducts the lesson by calling on various students, some with hands up, others seemingly at random from the nonvolunteers. (**Group alerting.**) About halfway through the exercises, a student enters the room and says that he is new to the school and has been assigned to the class. Mr. Case goes to his desk, sits down and says, "OK, come here. I'll check out some of your books to you. (**Lack of overlapping.**) I wish the school office wouldn't send children in the middle of the period. Where are you from anyway? That's a nice shirt you are wearing." (**Stimulus boundness.**) After finishing with the student and sending him to a seat, Mr. Case leaves his desk and says to the class, "Now where were we? Oh, yes, question 7. Say, where did Kim and Lee go? I didn't give them permission to leave." (**Lack of withitness.**) After several more minutes, Mr. Case calls a halt to the activity and says, "Now I'd like us to discuss the test coming up this Thursday. Let's make sure that you are all clear on what will be on the exam and what you will need to get ready for it." After a pause, he adds, "I almost forgot. Get your questions from before and look at the next to the last one. We need to add an important point that was left out . . . " After finishing the item, Mr. Case turns the topic back to the upcoming test. (**Flip-flop.**) "Now, where were we. Oh, yes. I need to show you some items that will be similar to those on the test. Here's one."

He writes it on the chalkboard, then pauses: "Well, I don't want to give away the test, do I?" Without discussing the test further, he turns to another topic. (**Dangle.**) "Just wait until you hear about the video tape we will be viewing tomorrow. I borrowed it from another teacher, and she said that her students thought it was one of the most interesting, exciting stories they had ever seen!" (**Group alerting.**)

CHAPTER 5

Case Study 5-1

Diagnosis. Although Ms. Lake has planned interesting presentations, her students seem to be floundering during the follow-up activities. A large part of Ms. Lake's problem lies with poor instructional clarity, poor sequencing of activities, and unclear directions. Students' poor showing on the five-item test suggests that related content from the previous week had not been understood. The twenty-minute presentation contains several indicators of poor clarity, including presenting information out of sequence, backtracking, inserting extraneous information, and moving from one topic to another without warning. In addition, the assignment does not support the content development activity. The assignment is made without checking for understanding and the directions are vague and indefinite.

Suggestions. Ms. Lake would achieve more success with her class if she concentrated on the following items:

- Information should be presented systematically; plan the lesson sequence and stick to it; state major goals and objectives; pace the lesson so that adequate time is available to cover major points; and avoid vagueness by being specific and using familiar words.

- Ms. Lake should review her procedures for keeping students responsible for work, especially in the areas of communicating work requirements and giving directions clearly. She should be sure that step-by-step directions are given for complex assignments, and she should ask students to repeat directions if there is a possibility that they do not understand them.

- During content development activities, frequent work samples should be obtained and other checks on student comprehension used. With this information, available instruction can be adjusted as needed.

- The amount of information being presented in any one lesson should be considered carefully. It might be better to present less information and leave sufficient time to check classwork prior to assigning students homework.

- Complex lessons should be broken down into smaller parts and later concepts should not be presented until primary ones are mastered.

- If some students still do not seem to understand after a presentation and discussion, the teacher can meet with them in a small group to review the presentation and answer questions. If one or two students consistently have difficulty, they can be seated near the teacher's desk so that it is easier to work with them.

- During the seatwork portion of lessons, the teacher should circulate to check student progress and to make sure that assignment directions are being followed.

CHAPTER 6

Problem 6-5

Diagnosis. Ms. Wade has failed to communicate and reinforce her expectations for classroom behavior and to establish rules and procedures that deal with the problem areas in her classroom. She apparently did not stop inappropriate behavior when it first began occurring; as a result, what could have been a good start during the first weeks of school has deteriorated into a difficult situation. At this point even the well-behaved students are misbehaving and her only deterrent has lost its effect.

Suggestions. Ms. Wade should decide what kinds of behavior she expects of her students, with regard to general conduct as well as procedures they should follow in particular activities. She should then develop new rules and procedures where they are needed and clarify and reteach those that were part of her original plan but are no longer effective. For example, she could set aside specific times for students to get drinks, use the restroom, sharpen pencils, or visit the class pets.

In addition, she should select a time—perhaps a Monday or the day after a school vacation—to introduce or to review and reteach the rules and procedures to her class. She should also explain to the students the rationales for the desired behaviors, and perhaps rehearse complex ones so that she can give students feedback about especially important behaviors. She will certainly want to review with the students when they may whisper quietly and when they must maintain silence. Because students have acquired some poor classroom talk habits, they may need visual cues such as stop or go signs to remind them when they must be silent and when they may whisper or talk in classroom voices. She can also help students learn when it is appropriate to talk quietly and when it is not, by alerting them about class noise level and encouraging them to monitor it themselves.

Ms. Wade should review procedures for working in small groups with the students. She may need to adopt the following practices:

- Use shorter seatwork periods, breaking up activities in the groups more often.

- Help students pace themselves by setting a timer to signal when work should be completed.

- Tell students ahead of time what work will be checked and when. Remind them that they will be questioned about their assignment when they come to the reading circle.

- Make sure that students in the first group understand their assignment by checking for understanding and having them do an example or two before calling for the second group.

- Monitor the out-of-group students for appropriate behavior while working with the reading group.

- After sending one group back to seatwork, don't call the second group until the work of the other students has been checked and help given when needed.

Once the rules and procedures are introduced—or reintroduced—to the class, Ms. Wade should:

- Monitor the class with the goal of anticipating and preventing misbehavior before it occurs and noting appropriate behavior.

- Make sure that students have enough work to do and that they understand and are able to complete tasks. Students should also know what specific things they can do when they have finished their assigned work.

- Structure some time for student movement and activity.

- Make statements that pace students through their work, such as: "You should now be working on problems 2 through 5. No one should be talking," or "After I've checked your paper you may go to the listening center."

- Reward academic performance and other desirable classroom behavior regularly, using stars, happy faces, displays of student work, pats on the back, smiles, etc.

- Be certain that stated consequences for inappropriate behavior are related to the misbehavior and that they can be carried out consistently. Positive consequences as well as negative ones should be communicated to students.

CHAPTER 7

Activity 7-2

1. b; 2. c; 3. d; 4. a; 5. c.

CHAPTER 9

Problem 9-1

The following approaches would help the team operate more smoothly:

- Strive for good cooperation and group planning among unit or team teachers. Each teacher must try to maintain the schedule. Have students watch the time. Post times for students to leave and list the materials they should take with them. Use a timer if necessary.

- Use established routines as much as possible for beginning and ending lessons; monitor the class to be sure students follow them.

- Teach students exactly what behaviors are expected during transitions; include expectations for voice level, use of the pencil sharpener, procedures for passing between classes, getting ready for the lesson, and so on.

- If early-arriving students are a problem, establish a "waiting area" where these students must wait quietly until the teacher can speak with them without interrupting the class.

- Use a short review activity or drill with the class or group while waiting for stragglers to arrive.

- Make sure students know what they are supposed to do when they return to the class. If they return while the teacher is conducting a lesson, give the group or the class a brief task to do while making sure students coming in get settled.

CHAPTER 9

Problem 9-2

Following are some specific suggestions for Ms. Ortiz:

- Each day, plan assignments that all students can complete, then provide supplementary assignments at different levels: enrichment and extension for faster students, review and practice assignments for slower students.

- Find out if any students in the class qualify for special assistance (such as special education resource room or bilingual tutoring).

- Use some small-group instruction in both reading and (at least temporarily) in mathematics. Be sure to keep groups flexible, changing membership according to achievement.

- Consider whether it might be possible to team with one or more teachers so that students on similar levels can be grouped for basic skills instruction.

- Consider the use of peer tutoring for certain activities and assignments.

- Share materials with other teachers to build a collection of supplementary materials above and below your grade level.

- Arrange student seating so that you have easy access to lower ability students and can monitor and help them readily during whole-class instruction.

- Be sure to include all students in class discussions and recitations. Do not let faster students answer most of the questions.

- After giving assignment directions to the whole class, check the lower ability students first to make sure they understand directions and are beginning work. If more than two or three students need further directions, meet with them immediately as a small group.

- When instructing the lower level students, break assignments and lessons into small segments and check frequently for understanding. Follow the suggestions for basic skill instruction presented in the section on teaching low ability students in Chapter 9.

References and Further Readings

Readers interested in other publications on classroom management by this book's authors and other writers in the field may choose from the following references.

Alberti, R. L., Ed. (1977). *Assertiveness: Innovations, applications, issues.* San Luis Obispo, CA: Impact Publishers.

Bandura, A. (1986). *Social foundations of thought and action.* Englewood Cliffs, NJ: Prentice-Hall, Inc.

Bassin, A., Bratter, E., & Rachin, R. Eds. (1976). *The Reality Therapy reader: A survey of the works of William Glasser.* New York: Harper & Row.

Brophy, J. (1981). Teacher praise: A functional analysis. *Review of Educational Research, 51,* 5–32.

Canter, L., & Canter, M. (1976). *Assertive discipline.* Santa Monica, CA: Canter and Associates, Inc.

Clements, B. S., & Evertson, C. M. (1982). *Orchestrating small group instruction in elementary school classrooms.* Austin, TX: Research and Development Center for Teacher Education (ERIC Document Reproduction Service No. ED 251 433).

Deci, E. L., & Ryan, R. M. (1985). *Intrinsic motivation and self-determination in human behavior.* New York: Plenum Press.

Doyle, W. (1986). Classroom management and organization. In M. Wittrock, Ed. *Handbook of research on teaching* (3rd ed., pp. 392–431). New York: Macmillan.

Dreikurs, R., Grunwald, B., & Pepper, F. (1982). *Maintaining sanity in the classroom: Classroom management techniques* (2nd ed.). New York: Harper & Row.

Duke, D. L., Ed. (1979). *Classroom management. The 78th Yearbook of the National Society for the Study of Education, Part II.* Chicago, IL: University of Chicago Press.

Duke, D. L., Ed. (1982). *Helping teachers manage classrooms.* Alexandria, VA: Association for Supervision and Curriculum Development.

Emmer, E. T. (1986). Academic activities and tasks in first-year teachers' classes. *Teaching and Teacher Education, 2,* 229–244.

Emmer, E. T. (1988). Classroom management and discipline. In V. Richardson-Koehler, Ed. *Educator's handbook: A research perspective (pp. 233–258).* New York: Longman.

Emmer, E. T. (1988). Praise and the instructional process. *Journal of Classroom Interaction, 23,* 32–39.

Emmer, E., & Aussiker, A. (1990). School and classroom discipline programs: How well do they work? In O. Moles, Ed. *Student discipline strategies: Research and practice (pp. 129–165).* Albany, NY: SUNY Press.

Emmer, E. T., & Evertson, C. M. (1981). Synthesis of research on classroom management. *Educational Leadership, 38,* 342–347.

Emmer, E. T., Evertson, C. M., & Anderson, L. M. (1980). Effective classroom management at the beginning of the school year. *Elementary School Journal, 80,* 219–231.

Emmer, E. T., Evertson, C. M., Clements, B. S., & Worsham, M. E. (1994). *Classroom management for secondary teachers* (3rd ed.). Boston: Allyn and Bacon.

Evertson, C. M. (1982). Differences in instructional activities in higher- and lower-achieving junior high English and math classes. *Elementary School Journal, 82,* 329–350.

Evertson, C. M. (1985). Training teachers in classroom management: An experimental study in secondary school classrooms. *Journal of Educational Research, 79,* 51–58.

Evertson, C. M. (1987). Managing classrooms: A framework for teachers. In D. Berliner & B. Rosenshine, Eds. *Talks to teachers (pp. 54–74).* New York: Random House.

Evertson, C. M., & Emmer, E. T. (1982). Effective management at the beginning of the school year in junior high classes. *Journal of Educational Psychology, 74,* 485–498.

Evertson, C. M., Emmer, E. T., Sanford, J. P., & Clements, B. S. (1983). Improving classroom management: An experiment in elementary school classrooms. *Elementary School Journal, 84*(2), 173–188.

Evertson, C. M., & Harris, A. H. (1992). What we know about managing classrooms. *Educational Leadership, 47*(7), 74–78.

Evertson, C. M., Sanford, J. P., & Emmer, E. T. (1981). Effects of class heterogeneity in junior high school. *American Educational Research Journal, 18,* 219–232.

Evertson, C. M., & Weade, R. (1989). Classroom management and teaching style: Instructional stability and variability in two junior high English classrooms. *Elementary School Journal, 89,* 379–393.

Foster, H. L. (1986). *Ribbin', jivin', and playin' the dozens: The persistent dilemma in our schools* (2nd ed.). Cambridge, MA: Ballinger Publishing Co.

Gazada, G. et al. (1991). *Human relations development: A manual for educators* (4th ed.). Boston: Allyn and Bacon.

Glasser, W. (1975). *Reality Therapy: A new approach to psychiatry.* New York: Harper & Row.

Glasser, W. (1977). 10 steps to good discipline. *Today's Education, 66,* 60–63.

Glasser, W. (1986). *Control theory in the classroom.* New York: Harper & Row.

Good, T. L., & Brophy, J. E. (1987). *Looking in classrooms* (4th ed.). New York: Harper & Row.

Gordon, T. (1974). *Teacher effectiveness training.* New York: Peter H. Wyden.

Johnson, D. W., & Johnson, R. T. (1991b). *Learning together and alone: Cooperative, competitive, and individualistic learning* (3rd ed.). Allyn and Bacon.

Jones, V., & Jones, L. (1990). *Comprehensive classroom management: Motivating and managing students.* (3rd ed.). Boston: Allyn and Bacon.

Kounin, J. S. (1970). *Discipline and group management in classrooms.* New York: Holt, Rinehart & Winston.

Kounin, J. S., & Gump, P. (1974). Signal systems of lesson settings and the task related behavior of preschool children. *Journal of Educational Psychology, 66,* 554–562.

Kounin, J. S., & Obradovic, S. (1968). Managing emotionally disturbed children in regular classrooms: A replication and extension. *Journal of Special Education, 2,* 129–135.

Lepper, M. R., & Greene, D., Eds. (1978). *The hidden costs of reward: New perspectives on the psychology of human motivation.* Hillsdale, NJ: Erlbaum.

Pitcher, G., & Poland, S. (1992). *Crisis intervention in the schools.* New York: Guilford Press.

Sanford, J. P., Clements, B. S., & Emmer, E. T. (1983). Improving classroom management. *Educational Leadership, 40,* 56–61.

Sanford, J. P., & Emmer, E. T. (1988). *Understanding classroom management: An observation guide.* Englewood Cliffs, N.J.: Prentice-Hall.

Sanford, J., & Evertson, C. (1980). Classroom management in a low SES junior high: Three case studies. *Journal of Teacher Education, 32*(1), 34–38.

Slavin, R. E. (1990). *Cooperative learning: Theory, research, and practice.* Allyn and Bacon.

Slavin, R., Sharan, S., Kagan, S., Hertz-Lazarowitz, R., Webb, C., & Schmuck, R., Eds. (1985). *Learning to cooperate, cooperating to learn.* New York: Plenum Press.

Stallings, J. A. (1977). *Learning to look: A handbook on classroom observation and teaching models.* Belmont, CA: Wadsworth Publishing Co.

Stoner, G., Shinn, M., & Walker, H. (1991). *Interventions for achievement and behavior problems.* Silver Spring, MD: National Association of School Psychologists.

Weade, R., & Evertson, C. (1988). The construction of lessons in effective and less effective classrooms. *Teaching and Teacher Education, 4,* 189–213.

Wolfgang, C., & Glickman, C. (1986). *Solving discipline problems* (2nd ed.). Boston, MA: Allyn and Bacon.

Zucker, E. (1983). *Mastering assertiveness skills: Power and positive influence at work.* New York: AMACON.

INDEX